# Nightmares and
# cold sweats

A Skill-Based Reading Anthology

Editorial Director: Susan C. Thies
Editor: Paula J. Reece
Contributing Writer: Laura Sauser
Book Design: Jann Williams
Production: Mark Hagenberg
Photo Research: Lisa Lorimor

**Image Credits:**
© Bettman/CORBIS: 51, 112, 129
© Robert Holmes/CORBIS: 75

Art Today: 8, 18, 25, 35, 38, 48, 65, 76, 88, 145, 164
Corbis: 4, 110–111
Mike Aspengren: 64, 97, 131, 153, 166
Sue Cornelison: 10, 95, 120
Photodisc: Cover, 6–7, 62–63

For information, contact
Perfection Learning® Corporation
1000 North Second Avenue, P.O. Box 500
Logan, Iowa 51546-0500.
Phone: 800-831-4190 • Fax: 800-543-2745
perfectionlearning.com

ISBN-10: 0-7891-5700-4  ISBN-13: 978-0-7891-5700-3
Printed in the U.S.A.

3 4 5 6 7 8 PP 13 12 11 10 09 08

# contents

# ghosts among the living

# The Adventure of the German Student

### Washington Irving

It was a stormy night during the violent times of the French Revolution. A young German was returning to his room at a late hour. He crossed the old part of Paris. The lightning gleamed. The loud claps of thunder rattled through the high, narrow streets. But let me first tell you something about this young German.

2 Gottfried Wolfgang was a young man of a good family. He had studied for some time at Göttingen, but he was a dreamer and an enthusiastic type. So he had wandered into wild and strange beliefs. Such thoughts have often confused other German students.

3 Wolfgang was lonely, and he worked very hard. His studies were unusual in nature. All of that affected both mind and body. In fact, his health was damaged, and his imagination was diseased. Strange spiritual ideas overtook him. Soon he had an ideal world of his own surrounding him.

4 He got the notion that there was an evil power hanging over him. I do not know what caused this idea. He thought that an evil spirit, or fiend, was trying to trap him—to make certain that his soul was lost.

5 Such an idea working on his unhappy nature produced the most gloomy effects. He became sickly and sad. His friends discovered the mental illness preying upon him. They decided that the best cure was a change of scenery. He was sent, therefore, to finish his studies among the wonders and joys of Paris.

6 Wolfgang arrived in Paris at the beginning of the revolution. At first, the popular madness caught his enthusiastic mind. He was delighted with the political and philosophical ideas of the day. But the scenes of

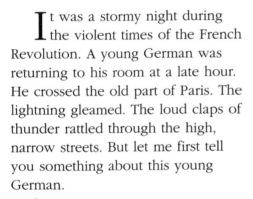

*Nightmares and Cold Sweats*

blood that followed shocked his sensitive nature. He became disgusted with society and the world. This made him withdraw from the world more than ever.

[7]He shut himself up in a lonely apartment in the Latin Quarter, the part of the city where students lived. It was a gloomy street. There he pursued his beliefs.

[8]Sometimes he spent hours at a time in the great libraries of Paris. They were like catacombs of departed authors. He dug through their piles of dusty and out-of-date works. He searched for food for his unhealthy appetite. He was, in a way, a literary ghoul. He fed on the decayed literature.

[9]Wolfgang, though lonely and alone, was of a fiery nature. For a time, this trait affected his imagination. But he was too shy and ignorant of the world to make any advances to the ladies.

[10]However, he was a passionate admirer of female beauty. In his lonely room, he would often lose himself in dreams about the many forms and faces he had seen. He conceived images of loveliness far greater than the real ones.

[11]While his mind was in this excited and weakened state, he had a dream. He dreamed of a female face of perfect beauty. Its effect upon him was so strong that he dreamed of it again and again. It haunted his thoughts by day and his sleep by night. In short, he fell passionately in love with this shadow of a dream.

[12]This lasted a very long time. It became one of those fixed ideas that haunt the minds of gloomy men. Such things are at times mistaken for madness.

[13]Such was Gottfried Wolfgang. And such was his life at the time I mentioned. He was returning home late one stormy night. He went through some of the old and gloomy streets of the ancient part of Paris.

[14]The loud claps of thunder rattled among the high houses of the narrow streets. Wolfgang came to the Place de Grève, the square where public executions were performed. The lightning trembled around the peaks of the ancient building behind the square. It shed flickering gleams over the open space in front.

[15]As Wolfgang was crossing the square, he shrank back in horror. He had found himself close to the guillotine. This dreadful tool of death stood ever ready. Its scaffold was always running with the blood of the good and the brave. It had,

*Wolfgang saw the very face that had haunted him in his dreams.*

that very day, been actively used in the work of murder. And there it stood in grim display. In a silent, sleeping city, it waited for fresh victims.

[16]Wolfgang's heart grew sick within him. He turned, shuddering, from the horrible machine. Then he saw a shadowy form. It cowered at the foot of the steps that led up to the scaffold.

[17]A series of bright flashes of lightning revealed it more clearly. It was a female figure, dressed in black. She was seated on one of the lower steps of the scaffold. She leaned forward, and her face was hidden in her lap. Her long hair hung to the ground, tangled and streaming with the rain that poured down.

[18]Wolfgang paused. There was something awful in this lonely monument of grief. The female had the look of being above the common class. Wolfgang knew the times to be full of change. Many a fair head that had once slept on a soft pillow now wandered the streets without a home.

[19]Perhaps this was some poor mourner who had been made lonely by the ax. Perhaps she sat here heartbroken. Perhaps all that was dear to her had been sent into eternity.

[20]He approached the woman and spoke to her in tones of sympathy. She raised her head and gazed wildly at him. He was filled with amazement at the face he saw by the bright glare of the lightning. It was the very face that had haunted him in his dreams. It was pale and unhappy, but thrillingly beautiful.

[21]Trembling with violent and confusing emotions, Wolfgang spoke to her again. He said something about her being unprotected at such an hour of the night. He spoke of

the fury of the storm and offered to lead her to her friends. She pointed to the guillotine with a gesture of dreadful meaning.

[22]"I have no friend on earth!" she said.

[23]"But you have a home," said Wolfgang.

[24]"Yes—in the grave!"

[25]The heart of the student melted at the words.

[26]"May a stranger dare make an offer," he said, "without danger of being misunderstood? I would offer my humble dwelling as a shelter and myself as a devoted friend. I am friendless in Paris and a stranger in the land. If my life could be of service, it is at your command. It would be sacrificed before harm or insult could come to you."

[27]There was an honest seriousness in the young man's manner that had its effect. His foreign accent, too, was in his favor. It showed him not to be the usual native of Paris. Indeed, there is an eloquence in true enthusiasm that cannot be doubted. The homeless stranger turned herself over completely to the protection of the student.

[28]The student led the woman through the ancient streets of the Latin Quarter. He took her to the great dingy hotel where he lived. The old woman doorkeeper who admitted them stared with surprise. It was an unusual sight to see the gloomy Wolfgang with a female companion.

[29]They entered his apartment. The student blushed at his bare and ordinary home. He had only one room—an old-fashioned living room. It had heavy, carved woodwork, and it was crazily furnished with the remains of former glory.

[30]This was one of those hotels in the area of the Luxembourg Palace that had once belonged to nobility. It was filled with books and papers and all the usual junk of a student. His bed stood in a recess at one end.

[31]When the lanterns were lit, the student had a better chance to see the stranger. He was positively drunk with her beauty. Her face was pale, but of a dazzling fairness. It was set off by full raven hair that clustered about it. Her large, bright eyes had an unusual, almost wild expression.

[32]As much as her black dress permitted her shape to be seen, her figure was of perfect balance. Her whole appearance was highly striking, though she was dressed in

the simplest style. She wore only one thing close to an ornament. That was a broad black band with a diamond clasp around her neck.

[33]The student now became perplexed about how to take care of the helpless being thus thrown upon his protection. He thought of leaving his room to her and seeking shelter elsewhere. Still, he was fascinated by her charms. There seemed to be a spell upon his thoughts and senses. He could not tear himself away from her presence.

[34]Her manner, too, was unusual and unexplained. She spoke no more of the guillotine. Her grief had stopped. The student's care had first won her trust. Then he had apparently won her heart. She seemed to be an enthusiastic type like he was. And such people soon understand each other.

[35]In the emotion of the moment, Wolfgang vowed his passion for her. He told her the story of his mysterious dream. He said that she had possessed his heart before he had ever seen her. She was strangely moved by his speech. She admitted to having felt drawn to him just as mysteriously.

[36]It was a time for wild theory and wild actions. Old prejudices and superstitions were done away with.

Everything was now under the rule of the "Goddess of Reason." Among other rubbish of the old times were the forms and ceremonies of marriage. They were considered too many ties for honorable minds. Social agreements were the style. Wolfgang was too much of a thinker to not be affected by the liberal beliefs of the day.

[37]"Why should we separate?" asked Wolfgang. "Our hearts are united. In the eye of reason and honor, we are as one. What need is there of earthly forms to bind high souls together?"

[38]The stranger listened with feeling. She must have been taught at the same school of thought.

[39]"You have no home or family," he continued. "Let me be everything to you. Or, rather, let us be everything to each other. If form is necessary, form shall be observed— there is my hand. I pledge myself to you forever."

[40]"Forever?" asked the stranger, solemnly.

[41]"Forever," repeated Wolfgang.

[42]The stranger clasped the hand held out to her. "Then I am yours," she murmured, and she sank upon his chest.

[43]The next morning, the student

left his bride sleeping. He set out at an early hour to seek more spacious apartments. He wanted something suitable to the change in his life. When he returned, he found the stranger lying with her head and one arm hanging over the bed.

[44]He spoke to her, but he received no reply. He went to wake her from her uneasy position. When he took her hand, it was cold—there was no pulse. Her face was pale and horrible. In a word, she was a corpse.

[45]Horrified and frantic, he called for help to everyone in the house. A scene of confusion followed. The police were sent for. As the police officer entered the room, he jumped back on seeing the corpse.

[46]"Great heaven!" he cried. "How did the woman come here?"

[47]"Do you know anything about her?" asked Wolfgang eagerly.

[48]"Do I!" cried the officer. "She was guillotined yesterday."

[49]He stepped forward. He undid the black collar around the neck of the corpse, and the head rolled onto the floor!

[50]The student burst into a frenzy. "The fiend! The fiend has gained possession of me!" he shrieked. "I am lost forever."

[51]They tried to soothe Wolfgang, but it was no use. He was taken with a frightful belief. He was sure that an evil spirit had brought the dead body back to life to trap him. He went insane and died in a madhouse.

---

*If you have been timing your reading speed for this story, record your time below.*

_____ : _____
   **Minutes**      **Seconds**

---

## UNDERSTANDING THE MAIN IDEA

The following questions will demonstrate your understanding of what the story is about, or the *main idea*. Choose the best answer for each question.

**1. This story is mainly about**

Ⓐ the French Revolution.

Ⓑ the guillotine and how it was used to punish criminals.

Ⓒ a man who withdrew from society and lived in a dream world.

Ⓓ a beautiful woman alone in Paris.

**2. This story could have been titled**

Ⓐ "The Bride."

Ⓑ "The Man Who Lost His Soul."

Ⓒ "The Mechanics of the Guillotine."

Ⓓ "Life During the French Revolution."

**3. Which detail best supports the main idea of the story?**

Ⓐ Wolfgang became convinced that a fiend was trying to trap him.

Ⓑ Many students studied in Paris.

Ⓒ The French Revolution was a time of wild theories and wild actions.

Ⓓ Wolfgang was a young man from a good family.

**4. Find another detail that supports the main idea of this story. Write it on the lines below.**

_____

_____

_____

_____

## RECALLING FACTS

The following questions will test how well you remember the facts in the story you just read. Choose the best answer for each question.

**1. Wolfgang's unusual studies**

Ⓐ affected his mind and his body.

Ⓑ challenged many German traditions.

Ⓒ won him many awards.

Ⓓ impressed his fellow students.

**2. While living in Paris, Wolfgang spent hours**

Ⓐ watching public executions.

Ⓑ studying with his friends.

Ⓒ searching through old books.

Ⓓ speaking out against the government.

**3. Wolfgang was haunted by thoughts and dreams of**

Ⓐ his family back in Germany.

Ⓑ the friends who had sent him to Paris.

Ⓒ a female face of perfect beauty.

Ⓓ old French authors.

**4. The woman at the guillotine told Wolfgang she**

Ⓐ had no friends and no home.

Ⓑ wanted to visit the great libraries with him.

Ⓒ had been executed that day.

Ⓓ was a fiend who wanted to steal his soul.

*Nightmares and Cold Sweats*

## READING BETWEEN THE LINES

A *theme* is a "message" found in a literary work. An *inference* is a conclusion drawn from facts. Analyze the story by choosing the best answer to each question below.

**1. A possible theme for this story is**

- Ⓐ withdrawing from the world can make you lose touch with reality.
- Ⓑ sometimes we all need a change of scenery.
- Ⓒ it's a good idea to get to know a woman before you marry her.
- Ⓓ the wild theories and actions of that time in history made people go mad.

**2. What conclusion can you draw from paragraphs 4–5?**

- Ⓐ Wolfgang's friends cared about his physical and mental health.
- Ⓑ Paris is a bad place to visit.
- Ⓒ Wolfgang didn't care what his friends thought of him.
- Ⓓ Wolfgang was forced to finish his studies.

**3. What conclusion can you draw from paragraphs 14–15?**

- Ⓐ Very few people were executed during that time.
- Ⓑ Many of the people executed during that time were innocent.
- Ⓒ Using the guillotine was a great way to control crime.
- Ⓓ Wolfgang enjoyed watching executions.

**4. It can be inferred from the story that**

- Ⓐ the French Revolution was a time of great change.
- Ⓑ Wolfgang's family and friends didn't approve of his new bride.
- Ⓒ Wolfgang and his bride decided not to go on a honeymoon.
- Ⓓ public executions were illegal.

## DETERMINING CAUSE AND EFFECT

Choose the best answer for the following questions to show the relationship between *what* happened in the story (*effects*) and *why* those things happened (*causes*).

**1. Because Wolfgang's friends sensed his mental illness, they**

Ⓐ sent him to Paris for a change of scenery.

Ⓑ called upon the finest doctors to examine him.

Ⓒ sentenced him to a public execution.

Ⓓ sent a beautiful woman to cheer him up.

**2. What happened because Wolfgang was too shy to make any advances to the ladies? Answer using complete sentences.**

_____

_____

_____

_____

_____

_____

**3. Why did Wolfgang offer to take the woman he met home?**

Ⓐ She told him she had no friends and no home.

Ⓑ He thought she seemed smart and interesting.

Ⓒ She seemed to share Wolfgang's political beliefs.

Ⓓ He wanted to save her from being executed.

**4. Why did the police officer jump back when he saw Wolfgang's dead lover?**

Ⓐ She was an old friend he hadn't seen in years.

Ⓑ He had never seen a corpse before.

Ⓒ He knew she had been guillotined the day before.

Ⓓ Like Wolfgang, he was in love with her beautiful face.

# USING CONTEXT CLUES

Skilled readers can often find the meaning of unfamiliar words by using *context clues*. This means they study the way the words are used in the text. Use the context clues in the excerpts below to determine the meaning of the **bold-faced** words. Then choose the answer that best matches the meaning of the word.

**1.** "[The libraries of Paris] were like **catacombs** of departed authors."

*CLUE*: "[Wolfgang] dug through their piles of dusty and out-of-date works. . . . He was, in a way, a literary ghoul. He fed on the decayed literature."

   Ⓐ catastrophes

   Ⓑ paradises

   Ⓒ tombs

   Ⓓ biographies

**2.** "[Wolfgang] **conceived** images of loveliness far greater than the real ones."

*CLUE*: "In his lonely room, he would often lose himself in dreams about the many forms and faces he had seen. . . . He dreamed of a female face of perfect beauty."

   Ⓐ imagined

   Ⓑ memorized

   Ⓒ purchased

   Ⓓ forgot

**3.** " 'I would offer my **humble** dwelling as a shelter and myself as a devoted friend.' "

*CLUE*: "The student blushed at his bare and ordinary home. He had only one room. . . ."

   Ⓐ fancy

   Ⓑ spacious

   Ⓒ furnished

   Ⓓ modest

**4.** "The student burst into a **frenzy**."

*CLUE*: " 'The fiend has gained possession of me!' [Wolfgang] shrieked. . . . They tried to soothe Wolfgang, but it was no use."

   Ⓐ calm mood

   Ⓑ state of joy

   Ⓒ fit of madness

   Ⓓ quiet rage

# The Signalman

### Charles Dickens

"Hello! Below there!"

When he heard a voice calling to him, he was standing at the door of his box. In his hands, he held a flag that was rolled around its short pole. One would have thought he would know where the voice came from.

I stood on the top of the steep hollow that was nearly over his head. But instead of looking up, he turned himself about and looked down the Line. There was something strange in the way he did so, but for the life of me, I could not decide what it was.

His figure looked shortened and shadowed down in the trench. And mine was high above him. I was soaked in the glow of an angry sunset. I had to shade my eyes to see him at all.

"Hello, below!"

He turned himself around again from looking down the Line. Raising his eyes, he saw my figure high above him.

"Is there any path by which I can come down and speak to you?"

He looked up at me without replying. I did not push him too soon by repeating my idle question. Just then came a vague shaking in the earth and air. It quickly changed to a violent throb. Then it became an oncoming rush that caused me to jump back. It felt like it had enough power to pull me down.

Steam rose to my height from this rapid train. It passed me and went racing over the landscape. As I looked down again, I saw him rolling up the flag he had shown while the train went by.

I repeated my call. He paused and stared at me. Then he motioned with his rolled-up flag toward a point on my level. It was some two or three hundred yards away.

*Nightmares and Cold Sweats*

[11]I called down to him, "All right!"

[12]I headed toward that point and looked carefully around. I found a rough zigzag path carved out. I followed it into the hollow.

[13]The hollow was very deep and unusually steep. It cut through a clammy stone that became oozier and wetter as I went down. For these reasons, I found the trip long. It gave me time to recall something strange about his attitude—he had looked unwilling to point out the path.

[14]When I came down low enough on the zigzag descent, I could see him again. He was standing between the rails of the track on which the train had just passed. He looked as if he was waiting for me to appear.

[15]He had his left hand at his chin. That left elbow rested on his right hand, which was crossed over his chest. His attitude was one of expectation and watchfulness. I stopped for a moment and wondered about it.

[16]I resumed my downward path. Stepping upon the level of the railroad, I drew near him. I saw that he was a very pale man; he seemed almost lifeless. He had a dark beard and rather heavy eyebrows.

[17]His post was in as lonely and dismal a place as I had ever seen. On either side was a dripping wet wall of jagged stone. The view to one side was just a crooked addition to this great pit. The shorter view was in the other direction. It ended in a gloomy red danger light that warned trains of the approaching tunnel. Next to it was an even gloomier entrance to a black tunnel. The huge tunnel had a forbidding look.

[18]Very little sunlight ever found its way to this spot. It had an earthy, deadly smell. A great deal of cold wind rushed through it. It chilled me, and I felt as if I had left the natural world for a moment.

[19]Before he stirred, I was near enough to touch him. Even then, he did not remove his eyes from mine. He took one step back and lifted his hand.

[20]This was a lonesome post to have, I said. It had caught my attention when I looked down from up yonder. A visitor was rare, I should suppose—and I hoped I wasn't unwelcome. I told him that I had been shut up within narrow limits all of my life. Since I had been at last set free, I had a newly awakened interest in seeing how things work.

[21]I know that I spoke to him of these things, but I am far from sure

of the words I used. I am not happy starting any conversation. And there was something about the man that disturbed me.

[22]He directed a curious look toward the red light near the tunnel's mouth. He looked all around it—for what, I do not know—and then he looked at me.

[23]"That light is part of your job, is it not?" I asked.

[24]He answered in a low voice, "Don't you know it is?"

[25]A horrible thought came to me as I studied his fixed eyes and gloomy face. I thought that this was a ghost, not a man. And I have wondered ever since whether there may have been an illness in his mind.

[26]At this thought, I stepped back. Then I saw a flash of fear in his eyes. This put my horrible thought into flight.

[27]I forced a smile. "You look at me," I said, "as if you were afraid of me."

[28]"I was wondering," he answered, "whether I had seen you before."

[29]"Where?"

[30]He pointed to the red light.

[31]"There?" I asked.

[32]Carefully watching me, he replied (but without sound), "Yes."

[33]"My good fellow, what would I do there? I never was—you may swear to it."

[34]"Yes, I am sure I may," he replied.

[35]His attitude cleared, as did my own. He now replied to my remarks with ease and eloquence.

[36]Had he much to do here?

[37]Yes. That was to say, he had enough responsibility to bear. Care and watchfulness were required of him. Of actual manual labor, he had next to none. He had to change that signal, to adjust those lights. He had to turn this iron handle now and then. That was all he had to do of that kind.

[38]He thought I seemed to make too much of those long and lonely hours. He could only say that the routine of his life had shaped itself into that form. He had grown used to it.

[39]He had taught himself a foreign language down here—that is, if knowing it only by sight could be considered learning it. (He had formed his own crude ideas of its sound.) He had also worked at mastering fractions and decimals. He had tried a little algebra. But he was, he said, a poor hand at figures.

*Nightmares and Cold Sweats*

[40]Was it necessary for him when on duty to remain in that hollow? Must he stay in that damp air? Could he never rise into the sunshine from between those high stone walls?

[41]Well, that depended upon circumstances. Under some conditions, there was less traffic on the Line than under others. The same held true for certain hours of the day and night.

[42]In good weather, he tried to find time to rise above these depths. But he was always likely to be called by his electric bell. At such times, he had to listen for it with double concern. So the relief was less than I would suppose.

[43]He took me into his box. There was a fire there. There was a desk for an official book in which he had to make certain entries. There was a telegraph. And there was the little bell he had spoken of.

[44]I trusted that he would excuse my saying that he had been well educated. I added that he was perhaps educated above this position. (I hoped I said this without insulting him.)

[45]He said that such occurrences were not rare, that they were often found in large groups of men. He said he had heard it was so in workhouses, the police force, and even in the army. And he knew it was so in any great railway staff.

[46]He said that he had once been a student of natural science. He had attended lectures. But he had run wild and misused his chances. He had slid down and never risen again. He had no complaint to offer about it. He had made his choices and was willing to live with the consequences.

[47]He said all of this in a quiet manner. His serious, dark glances were divided between the fire and me. He threw in the word *sir* from time to time, especially when he talked about his youth. He wanted me to understand that he claimed to be nothing but what I could see.

[48]He was interrupted several times by the little bell. Then he had to read off messages and send replies. Or he had to stand outside the door and display a flag as a train passed.

[49]He exchanged some words with the driver. In carrying out his duties, he was exact and alert. Several times he broke off his talk abruptly and remained silent until he had done what was needed.

[50]I should have considered this man one of the safest to hold that job. However, twice while speaking

to me, he stopped and became pale. He turned toward the little bell when it did not ring. He opened the door of the hut. He looked out toward the red light near the mouth of the tunnel. Both times he came back to the fire with a look I could not explain. It was the same look I had noticed when we were so far apart, and I had not been able to define it.

[51]When I rose to leave him, I said, "You almost make me think that I have met with a contented man."

[52](I must admit that I said this to lead him on.)

[53]"I believe I used to be," he replied in the low voice in which he had first spoken. "But I am troubled, sir, I am troubled."

[54]I could tell that he would have taken back the words if he could. But he had said them, and I took them up quickly.

[55]"What are you troubled by?"

[56]"It is very difficult to explain, sir. It is very, very difficult to speak of. But if you ever visit me again, I will try to tell you."

[57]"But I definitely intend to visit again. When shall it be?"

[58]"I shall be on again at ten tomorrow night, sir."

[59]"I will come at eleven."

[60]He thanked me and went out the door with me.

[61]"I'll show my white light, sir," he said in his strange low voice, "until you have found the way up. When you have found it, don't call out! And when you are at the top, don't call out!"

[62]His manner made the place feel colder. But I simply said, "Very well."

[63]"And when you come down tomorrow night, don't call out! Let me ask you a parting question. What made you cry, 'Hello, below there!' tonight?"

[64]"Heaven knows," I said. "I cried something like that—"

[65]"Not like that, sir. Those were the very words. I know them well."

[66]"I said them, no doubt, because I saw you below."

[67]"For no other reason?"

[68]"What other reason could I possibly have?"

[69]"You have no feeling that they were given to you in any supernatural way?"

[70]"No."

[71]He wished me good night and held up his light. I walked by the side of the rails until I found the path. (I had a very unpleasant

*Nightmares and Cold Sweats*

feeling that a train was coming behind me.) It was easier to climb than to descend. So I got back to my inn without any adventures.

[72]I was on time for my meeting the next night. I placed my foot on the first step of the zigzag path as the distant clocks were striking eleven. He was waiting for me at the bottom with his white light on.

[73]"I have not called out," I said, when we were close together. "May I speak now?"

[74]"Of course, sir."

[75]"Good evening, then, and here's my hand."

[76]"Good evening, sir, and here's mine."

[77]With that, we walked side by side to his box. We entered it, closed the door, and sat down by the fire.

[78]"I have made up my mind, sir," he began. He was bending forward and speaking only a little above a whisper. "You shall not have to ask me twice what troubles me. I took you for someone else yesterday evening. That troubles me."

[79]"That mistake?"

[80]"No. That someone else."

[81]"Who is it?"

[82]"I don't know."

[83]"Like me?"

[84]"I don't know. I never saw the face. The left arm is across the face, and the right arm is waved. Violently waved. This way."

[85]I followed his action with my eyes. It was the action of an arm gesturing with the greatest passion and force. It made me think of the words "For God's sake, clear the way!"

[86]"One moonlit night," said the man, "I was sitting here. I heard a voice cry, 'Hello, below there!' I jumped up and looked from that door. I saw him standing by the red light near the tunnel. He was waving as I just showed you. The voice seemed hoarse with shouting. It cried, 'Look out! Look out!' And then again, 'Hello, below there!'

[87]"I caught up my lamp and turned it on red. I ran toward the figure calling, 'What's wrong? What has happened? Where?' It stood just outside the blackness of the tunnel. I came so close to it that I had my hand stretched out to pull the sleeve away. Then it was gone."

[88]"Into the tunnel?" I asked.

[89]"No. I ran on into the tunnel, 500 yards. I stopped and held my lamp above my head. I saw the figures of the measured distance. I saw the wet stains stealing down the walls and trickling through the arch.

I ran out again, faster than I had run in. A mortal terror of the place had come over me.

[90]"I looked all around the red light with my own red light. I went up the iron ladder to the gallery on top of the tunnel. And I came down again and ran back here. I telegraphed both ways— 'An alarm has been given. Is anything wrong?' The answer came back, both ways— 'All is well.' "

[91]I resisted the slow touch of a frozen finger tracing my spine. I explained to him how this figure must have been a trick of his sense of sight.

[92]I told him about diseases of the delicate nerves that work the eye. Such figures were known to have troubled many patients.

[93]"As to an imaginary cry," I said, "listen for a moment to the wind in this unnatural valley. Do you hear the wild harp music it makes of the telegraph wires?"

[94]We sat listening for a while. That was all very well, he replied, but he ought to know something of the wind and the wires. He had often passed long winter nights here, alone and watching. Then he begged to say that he had not finished.

[95]I asked his pardon.

[96]Touching my arm, he slowly added these words, "Within six hours after the Appearance, the famous accident on this Line happened. Within ten hours, the dead and wounded were brought through the tunnel. They were carried over the spot where the figure had stood."

[97]A disagreeable shudder crept over me, but I did my best to fight it. It could not be denied. I replied that this was a remarkable coincidence. It was certain to affect him deeply. But it was true that remarkable coincidences happen constantly. And that they must be taken into account in dealing with such a subject.

[98]He again begged to say that he had not finished.

[99]I again begged his pardon for having interrupted again.

[100]"This was just a year ago," he said, placing his hand upon my arm. He glanced over his shoulder with hollow eyes. "Six or seven months passed, and I had recovered from the surprise and shock. Then I was standing at the door one morning. It was daybreak. I looked toward the red light and saw the ghost again."

[101]"Did it cry out?"

[102]"No. It was silent."

[103]"Did it wave its arm?"

[104]"No. It leaned against the shaft of the light with both hands before its face. Like this."

[105]Once more, I followed his action with my eyes. It was an action of mourning. I have seen such a pose in stone figures on tombs.

[106]"Did you go up to it?"

[107]"I came in and sat down, partly to collect my thoughts. It had made me feel faint. When I went to the door again, daylight was above me. And the ghost was gone."

[108]"But nothing followed? Nothing came of this?"

[109]He touched me on the arm with his forefinger three times. He gave a fearful nod each time.

[110]"Something happened that very day. As a train came out of the tunnel, I noticed something at a carriage window on my side. It looked like a confusion of hands and heads, and something waved. I saw it just in time to signal the driver—Stop!

[111]"He shut off and put his brake

*As a train came out of the tunnel, the driver was signaled to stop.*

on. But the train drifted past here 150 yards or more. I ran after it, and I heard terrible screams and cries. A beautiful young woman had died instantly in one of the rooms. She was brought in here and laid down on this floor between us."

[112]I pushed my chair back involuntarily. I looked at the floor and then at him.

[113]"True, sir. True. I tell it to you exactly as it happened."

[114]I could think of nothing to say that might help. My mouth was very dry. The wind and the wires took up the story with a long, sorrowful wail.

[115]He went on. "Now, sir, mark this and judge how my mind is troubled. The ghost came back a week ago. Ever since, it has been there now and again, by fits and starts."

[116]"At the light?"

[117]"At the Danger light."

[118]"What does it seem to do?"

[119]With great passion, he repeated that earlier gesture that made me think of "For God's sake, clear the way!"

[120]Then he went on. "I have no peace or rest from it. It calls to me in a tortured manner for many minutes at a time— 'Below there! Look out! Look out!' It stands waving

to me. It rings my little bell—"

[121]I stopped him at that. "Did it ring your bell yesterday evening when I was here? When you went to the door?"

[122]"Twice."

[123]"Why, see how your imagination misleads you?" I reasoned. "My eyes were on the bell, and my ears were open to the bell. And if I am a living man, it did not ring at those times. Nor at any other time. Not except when it was rung in the natural course of your everyday work. That was the station communicating with you."

[124]He shook his head. "I have never made a mistake about that, sir. I have never confused the ghost's ring with the man's. The ghost's ring is a strange vibration in the bell. It gets that sound from nothing else. And I have not said that the bell's vibration can be seen. I don't wonder that you failed to hear it. But I heard it."

[125]"And did the ghost seem to be there when you looked out?"

[126]"It was there."

[127]"Both times?"

[128]He repeated firmly, "Both times."

[129]"Will you come to the door

with me and look for it now?"

<sup>130</sup>He bit his lower lip. He seemed somewhat unwilling, but he arose. I opened the door and stood on the step while he stood in the doorway. There was the Danger light. There was the dismal mouth of the tunnel. There were the high stone walls of the hollow. There were the stars above them.

<sup>131</sup>"Do you see it?" I asked, taking careful note of his face. His eyes were big and strained—indeed, my own eyes had grown very large when I looked earnestly toward the same spot.

<sup>132</sup>"No," he answered. "It is not there."

<sup>133</sup>"Agreed," I said.

<sup>134</sup>We went in again, shut the door, and took our seats. I was thinking how best to improve on this progress, if it might be called that. Then he took up the conversation in a natural way. He seemed to assume that there could be no serious question of fact between us. I felt myself in the weakest of positions.

<sup>135</sup>"By this time, you will fully understand, sir," he said. "What troubles me so dreadfully is the question—what does the ghost mean?"

<sup>136</sup>I was not sure, I told him, that I fully understood.

<sup>137</sup>"What is it warning against?" he asked, thinking it over. His eyes were on the fire.

<sup>138</sup>"What is the danger? Where is the danger? There is danger hanging over us somewhere on the Line. Some dreadful calamity will happen. It is not to be doubted a third time. Not after what has already happened. But surely this is a cruel haunting of me. What can I do?"

<sup>139</sup>He pulled out his handkerchief and wiped the drops from his heated forehead.

<sup>140</sup>"I can telegraph to either side of me, or both. But if I telegraph 'Danger,' I can give no reason for it."

<sup>141</sup>He went on, wiping the palms of his hands. "I would get into trouble and do no good. They would think I was mad. This is the way it would work—Message: 'Danger! Take care!' Answer: 'What Danger? Where?' Message: 'Don't know. But for God's sake, take care!' They would replace me. What else could they do?"

<sup>142</sup>His pain of mind was most pitiful to see. It was the mental torture of a responsible man given more than he could bear. He was weighed down by a responsibility

that was impossible to figure out.

[143]"When it first stood under the Danger light, why did it not tell me?" he went on. He pushed his dark hair back from his face. He drew his hands across his temples in feverish worry.

[144]"Why didn't it tell me where the accident was to happen? Why didn't it tell me how it could be avoided? On its second coming, it hid its face. Why not tell me instead— 'She is going to die. Let them keep her at home'?

[145]"Perhaps it came on those two occasions only to show me that its warnings were true. If it wanted to prepare me for the third, why not warn me plainly now? And I, Lord help me! A mere signalman on this lonely station! Why not go to somebody higher up, somebody with the power to act?"

[146]When I saw him in this state, I saw what I had to do for the present. For the poor man's sake, as well as for the public's safety, I had to calm his mind. Therefore, I put aside all question of reality or unreality that stood between us.

[147]I told him that he must carry on with his duties. And that it should comfort him that he understood his duties. Even though

he did not understand these confusing appearances. I succeeded in this effort far better than in the attempt to reason him out of his beliefs. He became calm.

[148]As the night went on, the duties connected with his job began to make larger demands on his attention. I left him at two in the morning. I had offered to stay through the night, but he would not hear of it.

[149]I looked back at the red light more than once as I went up the pathway. I did not like the red light. I would have slept poorly if my bed had been under it. I see no reason to conceal any of this. Nor did I like the two events of the accident and the dead girl. I see no reason to conceal that, either.

[150]But what ran most in my thoughts was the question—How should I act? Something had been revealed to me. I had proved the man to be intelligent, watchful, careful, and exact. But in his state of mind, how long might he remain so?

[151]Though in a low position, he held a most important trust. Would I (for instance) like to stake my own life on him? What were the chances that he would continue to do his job well?

[152]I was unable to overcome a

feeling that there would be something disloyal in my telling what he had told me. I could not speak to his superiors in the company. First, I must be plain with him and propose a middle course.

[153] I finally decided to offer to go with him to the wisest medical doctor we could find in those parts. We would get the doctor's opinion. (Otherwise, I would keep his secret for the present.)

[154] He told me that a change in his work schedule would come around the next night. He would be off an hour or two after sunrise and on again soon after sunset. I made plans to return after sunset.

[155] The next evening was a lovely evening. I walked out early to enjoy it. The sun was not quite down when I crossed the path near the top of the deep hollow. I would extend my walk for an hour, I said to myself. It would then be time to go to my signalman's box.

[156] Before taking my stroll, I stepped to the edge. I unthinkingly looked down from the point from which I had first seen him. I cannot describe the chill that seized me. Near the mouth of the tunnel, I saw what appeared to be a man. His left sleeve was across his eyes. He was passionately waving his right arm.

[157] The nameless horror that weighed me down passed in a moment. For in a moment, I saw that what appeared to be a man was a man indeed. There was a little group of other men standing a short distance from him. The man seemed to be repeating the gesture he'd made before.

[158] The Danger light was not yet lighted. Against its pole was a little hut that was entirely new to me. It was made of some wooden supports and tarpaulin. It looked no bigger than a bed.

[159] I had an awful sense that something was wrong. I felt a flash of guilty fear that something fatal had come of my leaving the man there. I had not sent anyone to oversee or correct what he did. I proceeded down the worn path with all the speed I could manage.

[160] "What is the matter?" I asked the men.

[161] "Signalman killed this morning, sir."

[162] "Not the man belonging to that box?"

[163] "Yes, sir."

[164] "Not the man I know?"

[165] "You will recognize him, sir, if

you knew him," said the man who spoke for the others. He solemnly raised an end of the tarpaulin. "His face is quite intact."

[166]"Oh! How did this happen, how did this happen?" I asked. I turned from one to another as the hut was closed again.

[167]"He was cut down by an engine, sir. No man in England knew his work better. But somehow he was not clear of the outer rail. It was just at broad daylight. He had put out the light and had the lamp in his hand. As the engine came out of the tunnel, his back was toward her. She cut him down. This man drove her—show the gentleman how it happened, Tom."

[168]The man wore rough dark clothes. He stepped back to where he had been standing at the mouth of the tunnel.

[169]"Coming around the curve in the tunnel, sir," he said, "I saw him at the end. It was like seeing him through a spyglass. There was no time to cut speed, and I knew him to be very careful. Since he didn't seem to take heed of the whistle,

I shut it off. When we were running close to him, I called to him as loud as I could."

[170]"What did you say?"

[171]"I said, 'Below there! Look out! Look out! For God's sake, clear the way!' "

[172]I was startled.

[173]"Ah! It was a dreadful time, sir. I never stopped calling to him. I put this arm before my eyes so I would not see him. And I waved this arm to the last. But it was no use."

[174]I do not wish to make the story any longer or dwell on any one of its curious events more than on any other. But I will, in closing, point out a coincidence.

[175]The engine driver's warning included the words of the unlucky signalman. He had repeated them to me and said they haunted him. But the driver's warning also included my own words. He spoke the words that I myself—not the signalman—had given to the frantic gesture that the signalman had seen before. And I had said them only in my own mind.

---

*If you have been timing your reading speed for this story, record your time below.*

_____ : _____

**Minutes**     **Seconds**

---

*Nightmares and Cold Sweats*

## UNDERSTANDING THE MAIN IDEA

The following questions will demonstrate your understanding of what the story is about, or the *main idea*. Choose the best answer for each question.

**1. This story is mainly about**

Ⓐ the rules railroad conductors must follow to keep the railways safe.

Ⓑ the skills needed for a job in the railroad industry.

Ⓒ a signalman who saw a ghostly figure just before tragedy struck.

Ⓓ a friendship between two lonely people.

**2. This story could have been titled**

Ⓐ "Keeping the Rails Safe."

Ⓑ "An Unusual Friendship."

Ⓒ "Warning! Danger Ahead!"

Ⓓ "The Signalman's Lonely Job."

**3. Which detail best supports the main idea of the story?**

Ⓐ Just after the signalman saw the ghostly figure, a woman on the train died.

Ⓑ The signalman had once been a student of natural science.

Ⓒ The signalman's post was in a valley.

Ⓓ The narrator visited the signalman two days in a row.

**4. Find another detail that supports the main idea of this story. Write it on the lines below.**

_____

_____

## RECALLING FACTS

The following questions will test how well you remember the facts in the story you just read. Choose the best answer for each question.

**1. The signalman's post was**

Ⓐ in a dark, quiet hollow.

Ⓑ near a popular tourist spot.

Ⓒ close to a noisy city.

Ⓓ on the top of a mountain.

**2. During the lonely hours at his post, the signalman**

Ⓐ wrote songs about life on the railroad.

Ⓑ fell asleep on the job.

Ⓒ taught himself a foreign language.

Ⓓ talked to an imaginary friend.

**3. Within hours after the signalman saw the ghostly figure for the first time,**

Ⓐ he left work early.

Ⓑ a tragic train accident occurred.

Ⓒ he reported the event to the police.

Ⓓ he had his vision checked.

**4. The last time the figure appeared, it predicted**

Ⓐ a terrible storm.

Ⓑ a railroad workers' strike.

Ⓒ a fire that would destroy the hollow.

Ⓓ the signalman's own death.

## READING BETWEEN THE LINES

A *theme* is a "message" found in a literary work. An *inference* is a conclusion drawn from facts. Analyze the story by choosing the best answer to each question below.

**1. A theme for this story is**

&#9398; often, the lowest paying and lowliest jobs are the most important.

&#9399; traveling by rail can be dangerous.

&#9400; it can be hard to tell the difference between coincidences and supernatural events.

&#9401; no one can predict the future.

**2. What conclusion can you draw from paragraphs 90–93?**

&#9398; The narrator was trying to find a way to explain the signalman's story.

&#9399; The narrator had a medical background.

&#9400; The narrator was very angry with the signalman for lying.

&#9401; The narrator was making fun of the signalman's story.

**3. What conclusion can you draw from paragraphs 150–153? Answer using complete sentences.**

_____

_____

_____

_____

_____

_____

**4. It can be inferred from the story that the job of a railroad signalman**

&#9398; didn't allow many chances for making friends.

&#9399; was exciting and glamorous.

&#9400; was so busy, it left little time to daydream.

&#9401; was usually the first step to becoming a train conductor.

———————■———————

## DETERMINING CAUSE AND EFFECT

Choose the best answer for the following questions to show the relationship between *what* happened in the story (*effects*) and *why* those things happened (*causes*).

**1. Because the signalman had run wild and misused his chances when he was young,**

Ⓐ he had wound up in a position beneath his education.

Ⓑ his family had disowned him.

Ⓒ he spent all his time now entertaining friends.

Ⓓ he was rewarded with the position of signalman.

**2. What happened because the signalman told the narrator about the ghostly figure he'd seen?**

Ⓐ The narrator laughed at him.

Ⓑ The narrator tried to convince the signalman it was a trick of his senses.

Ⓒ The narrator tried to convince the signalman to tell his superiors.

Ⓓ The narrator got scared and ran away from the signalman's post.

**3. Why did the ghostly warnings upset the signalman so much?**

Ⓐ The signalman was very afraid of ghosts.

Ⓑ They meant something bad was going to happen and he couldn't prevent it.

Ⓒ They interrupted him while he was working, throwing his day off schedule.

Ⓓ They often woke him up in the middle of the night while he was trying to sleep.

**4. Why did the narrator decide not to go to the signalman's superiors about what the signalman told him?**

Ⓐ He figured it wasn't any of his business.

Ⓑ He thought the signalman was playing a joke on him.

Ⓒ He didn't think anyone would believe him.

Ⓓ He didn't want to be disloyal to his friend.

—————— ▬ ——————

# USING CONTEXT CLUES

Skilled readers can often find the meaning of unfamiliar words by using *context clues*. This means they study the way the words are used in the text. Use the context clues in the excerpts below to determine the meaning of the **bold-faced** words. Then choose the answer that best matches the meaning of the word.

**1.** "His post was in as lonely and **dismal** a place as I had ever seen."

*CLUE*: "On either side was a dripping wet wall of jagged stone. . . . Next to it was an even gloomier entrance to a black tunnel."

 Ⓐ colorful

 Ⓑ spiritual

 Ⓒ cheerful

 Ⓓ depressing

**2.** "He was **interrupted** several times by the little bell."

*CLUE*: "Then he had to read off messages and send replies. Or he had to stand outside the door and display a flag as a train passed."

 Ⓐ forgiven

 Ⓑ disturbed

 Ⓒ interested

 Ⓓ heard

**3.** "Some dreadful **calamity** will happen."

*CLUE*: "There is danger hanging over us somewhere on the Line."

 Ⓐ accident

 Ⓑ good fortune

 Ⓒ conversation

 Ⓓ gathering

**4.** "I was unable to overcome a feeling that there would be something **disloyal** in my telling what he had told me."

*CLUE*: "I could not speak to his superiors in the company. First, I must be plain with him and propose a middle course."

 Ⓐ selfless

 Ⓑ unfaithful

 Ⓒ unusual

 Ⓓ trustworthy

———— ▪ ————

*Nightmares and Cold Sweats*

# LESSON 3

# The *Queen Mary*

"It's still a very impressive ship," Bud Lewis remarked. He was standing on the deck of the *Queen Mary*, a grand old passenger liner that was now open to the public.

²"Yes, she is," the crewman replied. "She's big, luxurious . . ." He hesitated a moment, then grinned and said in a loud whisper, "And she's full of mysteries."

³Bud laughed. He'd been a newspaper reporter for five years, and he certainly didn't believe everything he heard. "I've been told that the *Queen Mary* is haunted," he said.

⁴The crewman's large dark eyes became serious. "Maybe haunted is the word for it," he said. "Or maybe she's just still inhabited by those who didn't want to leave. I couldn't say for sure. But I was told to show you around, Mr. Lewis, and let you decide for yourself."

⁵"That's very kind—uh, what was your name?"

⁶"You can just call me John," the crewman replied. He was a young dark-haired man with a pleasant expression. Even with his neatly trimmed beard, he looked like a teenager. Bud assumed that with the old ship permanently docked here in Long Beach, California, they no longer needed seasoned hands to keep her in shape.

⁷"Thanks, John," he replied. "Call me Bud, then."

⁸Bud followed the younger man's lead along the deck. In his blue coveralls, John looked more like a workman than a tour guide. Bud was pleased about that because someone who worked on the ship itself was likely to know a lot about it.

⁹The reporter's camera hung on a strap around his neck, and he carried a notebook in his hands. It was filled with news clippings, computer printouts, and his own handwritten notes. He'd hardly had time to glance at the stories about

the ship, but he'd go over them later.

[10]As they walked, Bud looked over his notes. The history of the ship was well known. The *Queen Mary* was a famous British ocean liner. She had been launched in 1934 and in 1938 had won an award for the fastest North Atlantic crossing of that time. Normally, she had carried more than 2,000 passengers and a crew of 1,100.

[11]During World War II, the *Queen Mary* had carried Allied troops instead of well-to-do passengers. She had been repainted a camouflage gray and nicknamed "The Grey Ghost." The ship had been just as successful at her new job. Adolf Hitler had offered a large reward and a medal to any submarine captain who could sink her.

[12]In 1967, the *Queen Mary* had been sent to Long Beach, California. Those interested in history, or in seeing how the wealthy used to travel, could visit her there. Tours were provided, but Bud had requested a more private viewing. He wanted to write about all the old ghost stories. That's why John had met him and was now guiding him around the old ship.

[13]They made their way through a central hallway that ran between first-class staterooms.

[14]"Some people say they've seen a ghost couple walking in this area. The well-dressed man and woman seem to be perfectly normal, but suddenly they disappear."

[15]John opened the door to a fancy stateroom. "Odd things have happened in some of these rooms," he said. "Lights suddenly turning themselves on or off, phones ringing with no one calling. Sleepers have been awakened by someone pulling on their sheets or breathing heavily nearby. When they turned on a light, no one else was in the room.

[16]"One tour guide even saw someone in a mirror that wasn't him or anyone in his group. The man in the mirror was dressed in a very old-fashioned suit—from the 1930s, I think he said."

[17]John opened another stateroom door. "This is the room that Winston Churchill used. Some say they can still smell the smoke of Churchill's favorite Cuban cigars in there."

[18]Bud checked out the room but didn't smell Churchill's cigar or anything else.

[19]Opening another door, John continued, "A woman was murdered in this room. But the man the

steward had seen her with was nowhere to be found. The room wasn't assigned to anybody, and no luggage was found in it or in the storage area. The funny thing was, several people remembered the man. They even remembered him checking in his luggage."

[20]Bud photographed the hallway and a couple of the staterooms, but he had to admit that he felt a bit disappointed. There was nothing in any of those places to even suggest a ghost. How could the passengers have imagined so much from absolutely nothing?

[21]He pulled out his notebook and jotted down a few words. As he followed John, he started flipping through the news stories to see if anything more interesting might be ahead.

[22]"More than 30 different artists worked on this ship," John said. "Painters, sculptors, metalworkers, and woodworkers. And they used more than 30 different kinds of wood to decorate the ship."

[23]Bud looked up from his notes. They were standing in the entrance to a large, richly decorated room. He shut his notebook and ran one hand along the smooth maple veneer on a nearby wall.

[24]"This is the first-class lounge,"

John said. Gesturing upward with one hand, he added, "It's three decks high. All the most elegant entertainments were held here. Just imagine it filled with the wealthy in their fancy gowns and jewels and formal tuxedos."

[25]Bud followed as John crossed the room. "At these tables they ate superb food and drank fine wines. And over here is the dance floor."

[26]Bud had to admit, it wasn't hard to imagine the chattering of happy and well-to-do travelers. In his mind, he could picture couples dancing to the music of an excellent band.

[27]"Here, some people have glimpsed a mysterious woman," John said. "She wears a white evening gown and dances all alone when the room is not brightly lit. They say she's keeping time to music that no one else can hear. Of course, not everyone sees her."

[28]"Have you seen her?" asked Bud.

[29]John ignored the question. "Once a small child in a tour group saw her," he said. "The little girl was standing right here. She kept pointing to that corner of the room and asking things like 'Why is she dancing all by herself?' and 'Why is she so dressed up?' The tour guide couldn't

*A mysterious woman danced to music no one else could hear.*

see anybody there, and neither could anyone else. But a few others have described the same vision."

[30]Bud stared into the shadows but saw nothing unusual. Finally, he shrugged his shoulders, lifted his camera, and took a picture of the corner. Then, just as he lowered the camera, he caught his breath. Had something moved? Had there been a brief swirl of white there in the corner?

[31]But of course, Bud told himself, he must have been mistaken. Nothing was moving there now.

[32]John, who had been watching the reporter carefully, turned and led the way out of the lounge. He added, "Sometimes the woman in white has been seen in other places too. Out here in the hallway and down by the first-class swimming pool. They say she looks quite normal except for her fancy gown. Sometimes she looks right at the person who spots her. Then she walks behind something, such as a column, and never comes out the other side. She just disappears."

[33]When Bud only grunted in reply, John changed the subject. "There are several restaurants and taverns on the ship," he said. "Those get a lot of poltergeist activity. You know the kind of stuff—dishes flying across the room, tables moving. It has scared a couple of the waitresses pretty badly."

[34]When Bud just looked bored,

    *Nightmares and Cold Sweats*

John tried another story. "Let's go up to the bow," he said. Bud followed him down a flight of stairs and toward the front of the ship.

[35]"Odd things have been heard or seen on all of the eight stories in the bow. Sometimes the crew quarters in this part of the ship have turned deathly cold. Other times people have heard—"

[36]"Voices!" said Bud. "Be quiet a minute."

[37]Both men stood quietly but heard nothing.

[38]"I could have sworn I heard—" Bud said, then stopped in midsentence. "There it is again."

[39]"Screams?" asked John.

[40]"Maybe," said Bud. "It might have sounded a little like men screaming."

[41]"Water pouring in?" asked John.

[42]Bud nodded. Then he said, "But it was only for a moment. It must have been my imagination."

[43]"I'm sure it was," said John. "But there is a reason why people might hear those sounds in this part of the ship. Sounds of water rushing in, sounds of men dying. It actually happened."

[44]"I remember reading something about that," Bud said. "The *Queen Mary* rammed another boat, didn't she? During the war?"

[45]"Yes, in 1942. The *Queen Mary* was carrying American troops to the war in Europe. Several British destroyers were patrolling the water ahead, because lots of German submarines were looking for her. An antiaircraft cruiser was sticking close to the *Queen Mary*. Too close, as it turned out."

[46]John stopped for a moment, as though the story was hard to tell. "The cruiser, named the *Coracoa*, zigzagged back and forth in front of the *Queen Mary*. Somehow, the pilot misjudged. The *Coracoa* cut too close, and the *Queen Mary* rammed her. The cruiser was cut in half and sank in less than five minutes. Water rushed into the *Queen Mary* through a gash in her bow, but it was easily stopped by closing watertight doors."

[47]Bud nodded, remembering the story now. "And the worst part was that the *Queen Mary* couldn't even pick up the survivors. It was against all regulations to bring such a huge ship to a stop. It would make her an easy target, and she was carrying thousands of men."

[48]"That's right," John said. "More than 300 men were drowned. Only 101 survived. Sometimes people hear the whole thing, as though it's

happening all over again."

[49]Bud stood silently and listened. There were no sounds at all. The *Queen Mary* was moored to the dock with permanent cables and gangplanks. No water could be rushing in. No men could be screaming from the water around the bow. It had been just his imagination after all. He made a few notes but found nothing to photograph.

[50]Bud checked his notebook again. "What about the swimming pool? I hear that some of the most interesting things have happened there."

[51]The first-class swimming pool became their next stop. It was not out in the open, like pools on ships that sailed the more southern waters. The *Queen Mary* was built to cross the cold and often dreary North Atlantic, and swimmers had to be kept warm. That's why the pool was deep within the ship.

[52]Bud and John stood in the entranceway, overlooking the area. The room was the size of a gymnasium, with thick columns holding up the ceiling. The area was softly lit, but even in the dim light, Bud could see that the walls were heavily decorated.

[53]Two stairways led down to the pool deck below. The pool was half full of water.

[54]"Do people still swim here?" Bud asked.

[55]"No one's allowed to use the pool," John replied. "Some water is kept in it to help prevent cracking."

[56]As they started down one of the stairways, Bud watched the nearest columns closely. If a lady in a white dress was walking around down there, he didn't want to miss her. If she was, he'd bet that she would turn out to be a regular flesh-and-blood person who could be caught and questioned. And that sort of thing was his job, after all.

[57]That's why he wasn't looking in the direction of the splash that came from the other end of the pool. Bud's head jerked around. Yes, the water at that end was still rolling a little. But he couldn't see what had gone into or out of the water, making that sound.

[58]Followed by John, Bud hurried around to that end of the pool. He could see no one there. But he did see something else.

[59]"Hah!" Bud cried. "I don't think ghosts leave footprints." He pointed at the clear, wet marks leading away from the water.

[60]"Maybe we'd better follow

them," John suggested.

[61]The footprints led all the way around the pool—and back to the stairway the two men had just come down! Bud frowned and stared around the room. No one could have taken that route without being seen. And yet, he had seen no one.

[62]He went back to trace the steps again, but the footprints were gone. How could the wet footprints have dried so quickly? Puzzled, Bud returned to the stairway. Now there were wet footprints going up the stairs. He dashed upward but found no one at the top. When he looked back, he saw that the wet footprints had already disappeared from the stairs.

[63]John also climbed the staircase out of the pool area. Grumpily, Bud refused to try to find the disappearing trail. It must be some kind of trick, he decided. And he'd been fooled enough already. Then Bud realized that he hadn't even taken pictures of the prints. If he wrote about this, no one would ever believe him.

[64]"Somebody's having a good laugh on us," Bud grumbled.

[65]"Maybe," said John. "But there's an alarm that goes off when anyone goes into the pool area who's not supposed to be there. I shut it off just before the two of us went in. But it should have let us know if anyone was there ahead of us."

[66]"I still think you have a practical joker on board who likes to swim," Bud complained.

[67]John grinned. "Well, I can only tell you what a certain psychic claims," he said. "Lots of different sightings have happened in the pool area—a couple of children, a guy or two from troops that were bunked here, and, of course, the lady in white. This psychic lady talked about it on TV. She said there's a vortex in this area."

[68]"What do you mean, a vortex?" demanded Bud. "What kind of vortex?"

[69]"Well, it's a strange power point. Sometimes living people have trouble walking through a certain spot. The sensation is so weird, it frightens them. That's the vortex. Sometimes it won't let the living through at all."

[70]"I didn't feel anything like that," Bud protested.

[71]"Not everyone does," said John. "But the psychic claimed that a vortex allows spirits from other places to enter here."

[72]"In other words," Bud asked,

"the *Queen Mary* could be haunted by ghosts from other places, as well as those from the ship?"

[73]"That's what she said," John replied. When Bud didn't respond to that idea, John suggested, "Now let me show you the place I like best."

[74]Bud followed John down more stairs and into a long space lined with numbered doors. A catwalk ran along between the doors, past the two engine rooms, and to the ship's great propeller shaft. A few oil drums were near the catwalk, and a number of chains hung overhead.

[75]John led the way along the catwalk. Bud took some pictures of the area, just because it was interesting to see. But as they came near a door with the number 13 on it, he almost dropped his camera.

[76]"Look out!" Bud cried.

[77]Door number 13 was on fire! Flames shot out of the metal surface, and smoke was pouring across the catwalk. For some reason, John didn't seem to be paying any attention to it.

[78]"There's a particular ghost people often meet on this ship," John said. "A young man who died here."

[79]John's voice was so solemn that Bud couldn't help listening, in spite of the nearby flames.

[80]"He died trying to escape from a fire," John said. "He was still just a teenager."

[81]And with that, John turned and faced door number 13. Bud stared as his guide began to fade from view. Was it because of the smoke?

[82]But as Bud watched, John disappeared completely. Bud gasped and whirled around to see if John was somewhere else in the area. When he looked back at door number 13, Bud again saw the young man in the blue coveralls. He was walking directly into the fire!

[83]"John!" Bud cried.

[84]But John didn't stop. He walked straight ahead into the flames—and through the closed metal door. Then a horrible scream rang through the area.

[85]Bud's knees buckled, and he thought he might faint. But then he saw that the flames were gone. The smoke was gone. And John had vanished too.

[86]A young man, Bud thought. A teenager.

[87]He pulled out his notebook and clawed through the stories about the *Queen Mary*. And there it was. A young man named John Pedar had died trying to escape from a fire. He

had been crushed to death by a closing door.

[88]John Pedar was described as a bearded young man, 18 years old, with dark hair and brown eyes.

[89]Bud Lewis scrambled up stairways and down hallways until he found his way out of the *Queen Mary*. He never did write his story about the haunted ship. After all, he had no pictures of the strange happenings. So who would believe him?

---

*If you have been timing your reading speed for this story, record your time below.*

_____ : _____

**Minutes     Seconds**

## UNDERSTANDING THE MAIN IDEA

The following questions will demonstrate your understanding of what the story is about, or the *main idea*. Choose the best answer for each question.

**1. This story is mainly about**

&#9398; a haunted ocean liner.

&#9399; a young man's tragic death.

&#9400; how ocean liners were used during World War II.

&#9401; tourist attractions in California.

**2. This story could have been titled**

&#9398; "Where to Go in California."

&#9399; "Too Young to Die."

&#9400; "The Ghost Ship."

&#9401; "The History of the Ocean Liner."

**3. Which detail best supports the main idea of the story?**

&#9398; John explained that there had been a number of unexplained events on the *Queen Mary*.

&#9399; John told Bud that no one was allowed to use the pool, but some water was kept in it to keep it from cracking.

&#9400; Bud was a newspaper reporter.

&#9401; The *Queen Mary* was sent to Long Beach, California, in 1967.

**4. Find another detail that supports the main idea of this story. Write it on the lines below.**

_____

_____

_____

## RECALLING FACTS

The following questions will test how well you remember the facts in the story you just read. Choose the best answer for each question.

**1. During World War II, the *Queen Mary***

&#9398; became a popular tourist attraction.

&#9399; had many famous guests on board.

&#9400; was Adolf Hitler's favorite ship.

&#9401; carried Allied troops.

**2. According to John, one of the ship's ghost stories involved**

&#9398; a mysterious woman in a white dress.

&#9399; a newspaper reporter.

&#9400; a birthday party.

&#9401; people playing cards.

**3. A psychic claimed the pool area had a vortex which**

&#9398; frightened away evil spirits.

&#9399; allowed spirits from other places to enter.

&#9400; attracted the ghosts of the rich and famous.

&#9401; made the pool too dangerous to swim in.

**4. John the tour guide was really**

&#9398; the woman in the white dress.

&#9399; a teenager who died on the ship.

&#9400; an undercover reporter.

&#9401; the ship's former captain.

*Nightmares and Cold Sweats*

## READING BETWEEN THE LINES

A *theme* is a "message" found in a literary work. An *inference* is a conclusion drawn from facts. Analyze the story by choosing the best answer to each question below.

**1. A theme for this story is**

Ⓐ sometimes people are not who they seem to be.

Ⓑ there is a practical explanation for everything.

Ⓒ supernatural beings are not dangerous.

Ⓓ believing in ghosts is a waste of time.

**2. What conclusion can you draw from paragraphs 45–48?**

Ⓐ The lives of the *Coracoa* crew were sacrificed to protect the crew of the *Queen Mary*.

Ⓑ The crew of the *Queen Mary* didn't care about the men on the *Coracoa*.

Ⓒ The collision between the two ships was not an accident.

Ⓓ The *Coracoa* was a well-built ship.

**3. What conclusion can you draw from paragraph 56?**

Ⓐ Bud's job was to give tours of the *Queen Mary*.

Ⓑ Bud was frightened of ghosts.

Ⓒ Bud wanted to prove the ghost stories weren't real.

Ⓓ The woman in the white dress wanted to meet Bud.

**4. It can be inferred from the story that**

Ⓐ many people who have visited the *Queen Mary* now believe in ghosts.

Ⓑ the *Queen Mary* is a nice place for ghosts to visit.

Ⓒ John Pedar is a popular tour guide.

Ⓓ all of the strange events on the *Queen Mary* have been practical jokes.

---

## DETERMINING CAUSE AND EFFECT

Choose the best answer for the following questions to show the relationship between *what* happened in the story (*effects*) and *why* those things happened (*causes*).

**1. Because there have been many unexplained events on the *Queen Mary*,**

Ⓐ it has been closed to the public.

Ⓑ it was permanently docked in Long Beach, California.

Ⓒ it has been nicknamed the "Floating House of Horrors."

Ⓓ people believe it is haunted.

**2. On the lines below, write the effect for the following cause in the story.**

*CAUSE*: The *Queen Mary* rammed into the *Coracoa*.

*EFFECT*:

_____

_____

_____

_____

**3. Why was the *Queen Mary* nicknamed the Grey Ghost during World War II?**

Ⓐ It was repainted camouflage gray.

Ⓑ The ship would often mysteriously disappear while out on the water.

Ⓒ The soldiers on board reported lots of unexplained events.

Ⓓ The Allied soldiers wore gray uniforms.

**4. Why didn't Bud write his story about the haunted ship?**

Ⓐ He promised John he'd keep it a secret.

Ⓑ He was too afraid to write about it.

Ⓒ He had no pictures to prove what he'd seen.

Ⓓ He couldn't remember what happened.

———— ▬ ————

## USING CONTEXT CLUES

Skilled readers can often find the meaning of unfamiliar words by using *context clues*. This means they study the way the words are used in the text. Use the context clue in the excerpts below to determine the meaning of the **bold-faced** words. Then choose the answer that best matches the meaning of the word.

**1.** " 'It's still a very **impressive** ship,' Bud Lewis remarked."

*CLUE*: "He was standing on the deck of the *Queen Mary*, a grand, old passenger liner. . . . 'She's big, luxurious . . .' "

Ⓐ ordinary

Ⓑ tasteless

Ⓒ useful

Ⓓ outstanding

**2.** "Bud assumed that with the old ship permanently docked here in Long Beach, California, they no longer needed **seasoned** hands to keep her in shape."

*CLUE*: "Even with his neatly trimmed beard, [John] looked like a teenager."

Ⓐ experienced

Ⓑ fresh

Ⓒ young

Ⓓ immature

**3.** " 'All the most **elegant** entertainments were held here.' "

*CLUE*: " 'Just imagine it filled with the wealthy in their fancy gowns and jewels and formal tuxedos.' "

Ⓐ grand

Ⓑ crude

Ⓒ casual

Ⓓ frightening

**4.** "John's voice was so **solemn** that Bud couldn't help listening, in spite of the nearby flames."

*CLUE*: " 'He died trying to escape from a fire,' John said. 'He was still just a teenager.' "

Ⓐ quiet

Ⓑ happy

Ⓒ silly

Ⓓ serious

---

# A Mansion Built for Ghosts

In the mid-1800s in New Haven, Connecticut, there lived a beautiful young woman. At four feet ten inches tall, Sarah was not only beautiful, but charming, musically talented, and proficient in several languages. She was very popular in New Haven society.

[2] Sarah soon focused her attention on a young New Haven man. And in 1862 the couple married. The Civil War was raging at the time, tearing families apart and ruining lives. However, this couple was one of the few who actually benefited from the war.

[3] The groom was William Wirt Winchester. From his father, he inherited a company that manufactured guns. In fact, William produced the first rifle that could fire rapid shots one after another—the first true repeating rifle. By the start of the Civil War, that rifle was in great demand by the Northern army. Between government contracts and individual sales, money poured into the Winchester Repeating Arms Company.

[4] In 1866, Sarah gave birth to a daughter, but the child died before a month had passed. Nearly insane with grief, Sarah withdrew from society, even from her family. It was nearly ten years before she seemed ready to regain a normal life.

[5] But then tragedy struck again. In 1881, William died from tuberculosis. Sarah again retreated into her sorrow. She inherited incredible wealth, but that did nothing to ease her pain. Her friends tried to get her to rejoin society to no avail.

[6] Only one of Sarah's former interests remained. She was still fascinated by spiritualism—the idea that certain people could contact the spirits of the dead. At that time, many people believed that a psychic called a medium could enter into a trance and communicate with those who were no longer living.

[7] Spiritualism had been very popular in America for about 40

years. The craze was started in 1848 by a young woman named Margaret Fox and her two sisters. They began inviting people to meetings in their old New York farmhouse, which was rumored to be haunted. The visitors asked questions, and spirits answered with rapping noises. Many people were convinced that they were communicating with dead relatives and friends through the Fox sisters.

[8]The Fox family moved to Rochester, New York, and continued gathering people together to hear their rapping spirits. The sisters soon became famous both in the States and in Europe. They toured the country with P. T. Barnum, holding popular séances. By the mid-1850s many other psychics also said they were contacting the spirits of the dead. They went into trances and spoke in mysterious voices, levitated tables, and manifested visible ghosts.

[9]In the late 19th and early 20th centuries, many people believed in these mediums and séances. Among the believers were American journalist Horace Greeley and British author Sir Arthur Conan Doyle. However, Doyle's own fictional creation, Sherlock Holmes, would have been much more skeptical about the whole thing.

[10]Later in life, Margaret Fox converted to Roman Catholicism and insisted that the séances had been a hoax. She said that she had produced the rapping noises by manipulating her own joints. But by then, many people were spiritualists, and they didn't accept Margaret's change of story. In fact, she did later return to spiritualism to make her living.

[11]At the time that Sarah Winchester lost her husband, many popular mediums were holding séances. When a friend of Sarah's suggested they attend a séance to be held by a medium from Boston, Sarah agreed to go. Perhaps the man would be able to tell her something about the loved ones she had lost.

[12]Sarah and her friend entered the dark room where the séance was to take place. Black curtains covered the windows, preventing any outside light from penetrating the darkness. In the middle of the room stood a stark table. Several candlesticks supporting white pillars of wax were placed upon the tabletop. Sarah noted that, despite the fact that they produced heat, the candles themselves had a cold look to them.

[13]The medium invited Sarah and her friend to sit down. Several other men and women were already seated around the large, dark table. They glanced at Sarah and her friend

and then returned to their thoughts. Sarah thought that they all looked ready, yet unprepared. Excited, yet frightened. Exactly as she felt.

[14]When the séance began, the medium contacted a few family members and long lost loves of others at the table. Sarah began to get restless. She had come to the séance with high hopes in her heart. She was hoping she would hear something—anything—that related to her loved ones.

[15]Suddenly the medium addressed Sarah.

[16]"The spirit of your husband is standing beside you," he said.

[17]Sarah felt the hairs bristle on the back of her neck. She, at first hesitantly, then eagerly, looked beside her. She saw nothing.

[18]The medium sensed her doubt. He convinced Sarah by describing what her husband looked like. Then he said, "William has an important message for you."

[19]"What is it?" Sarah whispered.

[20]"The message is that your husband and child died because of a curse on your family. The ghosts of all those who have been killed by Winchester rifles have taken revenge on you," said the medium.

[21]So the powerful weapon had brought death upon its maker and his child. Now even his widow was threatened.

[22]"You must build a house," the medium instructed. "It must be a mansion large enough to hold all the spirits of the dead killed by the Winchester rifle. But it should not be here in Connecticut. You will be shown the place, and you will be told how to build it. As long as you are building this house, you will live. When you stop building it, you will die."

[23]Sarah sat in a state of shock. She didn't want to believe what she had heard. But yet—what if it were true? It did seem that her family had experienced its share of bad luck. Did a curse seem that far-fetched?

[24]But how can I be expected to build a house for all the spirits of the dead killed by the Winchester rifle? she thought. Hundreds were killed—no, surely there must have been thousands. How could I hope to house them all, to please them all, and to escape their fury?

[25]The medium once again sensed Sarah's anxiety.

[26]"Your husband will guide you," he said. "He will tell you exactly where to build."

[27]So Sarah went home and

waited for further instructions. But she wondered how those instructions would get to her. Would William leave a note? Would he send a messenger? Or would he appear himself, right in front of her face?

[28]One day Sarah had a sudden urge to move to California. Taking this as a sign from her husband, she sold her house in New Haven and traveled alone across the country. In the Santa Clara Valley of California, just south of San Francisco, she found what she was looking for.

*Sarah Winchester*

[29]In the town of San Jose, Sarah saw a large house under construction. Her dead husband's voice told her that this was the place she must build. The original plan called for 17 rooms, but the house would eventually have many more rooms than that. Sarah bought the house and land from its owner, then started giving new instructions to the builder.

[30]Her fortune allowed her to do whatever she wanted. According to the medium's instructions, someone had to be kept working 24 hours a day, every day of the year. She hired as many carpenters and other workers as she needed to keep the work going in shifts. The nonstop building went on for 36 years.

[31]The house changed constantly as Sarah had rooms built, then torn down to make way for new rooms. She had a tall hedge put around the property to hide the strange activity from those who passed by.

[32]She built a small, windowless room in which she held her own séances. Meeting there with her ghosts, she became convinced that good spirits were present as well as the evil ones that still wanted revenge. She had a bell tower put up, and every night a bell summoned the spirits at midnight. At 2 a.m. the

bell rang again, signaling that the séance was over. And each night, Sarah emerged from her hidden room with new plans for the next day's construction.

[33]The house that Sarah built grew year by year. By 1906, the house was seven stories tall. That year, the San Francisco earthquake damaged some of the rooms. Sarah was rescued from the house, but she was convinced that the evil ghosts had finally caught up with her. She had 30 rooms boarded up for good, including the one she had been sleeping in when the quake struck.

[34]Then she continued building, and she never stopped as long as she lived. Perhaps the house is so odd because she had to keep building for so long. But perhaps it was meant to be a puzzle, or even a trap for ghosts.

[35]The house does seem to have been designed to confuse someone or something. It has a multitude of staircases and hallways, secret passageways, and hidden rooms. Some windows don't lead outside, some doors lead to a blank wall, and other doors open to a sheer drop outside an upper floor. Some rooms were constructed around other rooms, while other rooms grew crazily into entire wings. The roof is a jumble of towers, turrets, and cupolas.

[36]Some stairways go up or down to dead ends. In other cases, rooms can be reached by taking one flight of stairs down and another back up. One stairway has 44 steps but only goes up ten feet to the next floor. Other stairs and some chimneys end halfway up a wall. There are three elevators, but one only goes up one floor.

[37]It is said that Sarah knew the house well. She used the secret ways to slip from room to room. She slept in a different bedroom every night so the ghosts couldn't find her. And she only entered her hidden séance room when she felt sure that the angry ghosts had lost her trail.

[38]At some point, Sarah must have become convinced that the number 13 would protect her. She built rooms with 13 windows, stairways with 13 steps, and 13 bathrooms in the house. She even ordered chandeliers made with 13 lights.

[39]She often held lavish banquets for 12 guests, making a total of 13 at the table. Although the food was real and quite excellent, Sarah was the only visible guest.

[40]In one sense, Sarah lived in the house alone. But of course there

were servants, as well as the constant parade of workers. Perhaps she also had occasional visitors. According to some stories, President Theodore Roosevelt visited Sarah—according to others, she turned him away. Others say that the magician Harry Houdini visited her.

[41]After a midnight séance in 1922, Sarah Winchester died in her sleep at the age of 83. When it was found that her bank account had dwindled away, rumors started that a fortune was hidden somewhere in the house. The treasure was said to include jewelry and a solid gold dinner service that Sarah had used to entertain the ghosts. No such things were ever found.

[42]Sarah stated in her will that her ghostly guests must always be welcome in the house. And it seems that they probably are. Visitors, employees, and especially visiting psychics often experience strange noises and sights—footsteps, banging doors or windows, voices, strange breathing, cold spots, moving lights, and doorknobs that turn by themselves. Lights go on and off by themselves; organ music plays without an organ. Even the smells of cooking come from an unused kitchen.

[43]Some visitors have had visions of a couple dressed as servants, visions of workers, and even visions of Sarah herself. Some claim to have taken photographs of Sarah. During one séance, a psychic seemed to age and take on Sarah's physical appearance.

[44]So perhaps Sarah herself still haunts her remarkable house. If so, let's hope she no longer has to flee the terrible spirits that haunted her life. Most likely she doesn't, since now she seems to delight in entertaining her human visitors. It is said that she is a gentle spirit and that no one need fear her.

*If you have been timing your reading speed for this story, record your time below.*

_____ : _____
**Minutes     Seconds**

## UNDERSTANDING THE MAIN IDEA

The following questions will demonstrate your understanding of what the story is about, or the *main idea*. Choose the best answer for each question.

**1. This story is mainly about**

  Ⓐ a woman who spent years trying to protect herself from a curse.

  Ⓑ how the Winchester rifle was used to defeat the South in the Civil War.

  Ⓒ séances and how they became popular in America.

  Ⓓ Californians in the early 1900s.

**2. This story could have been titled**

  Ⓐ "Turn-of-the-Century Californians."

  Ⓑ "The History of the Winchester Repeating Arms Company."

  Ⓒ "The Winchester Family Curse."

  Ⓓ "How to Hold a Séance."

**3. Which detail best supports the main idea of the story?**

  Ⓐ Sarah kept workers building and rebuilding her house nonstop for 36 years.

  Ⓑ Sarah's fortune allowed her to do whatever she wanted.

  Ⓒ Sarah Winchester died in her sleep at the age of 83.

  Ⓓ Sarah's only child died before the infant was even a month old.

**4. Find another detail that supports the main idea of this story. Write it on the lines below.**

_____

_____

_____

## RECALLING FACTS

The following questions will test how well you remember the facts in the story you just read. Choose the best answer for each question.

**1. The Winchester family made its fortune by**

  Ⓐ hosting parties for New Haven society.

  Ⓑ building and remodeling houses.

  Ⓒ conducting séances.

  Ⓓ manufacturing guns.

**2. After her husband and daughter died, Sarah became fascinated with**

  Ⓐ contacting the dead.

  Ⓑ spending her fortune.

  Ⓒ running the family business.

  Ⓓ finding a new husband.

**3. Later in life, Margaret Fox confessed that her séances were**

  Ⓐ the only sure way to contact the dead.

  Ⓑ the reason she was afraid of ghosts.

  Ⓒ only a hoax.

  Ⓓ not as difficult to perform as they looked.

**4. The medium told Sarah she must build a house large enough to hold**

  Ⓐ the spirits of the dead killed by the Winchester rifle.

  Ⓑ weekly séances for her friends.

  Ⓒ all of Sarah's relatives, including her cousins.

  Ⓓ large parties for the rich and famous of society.

*Nightmares and Cold Sweats*

## READING BETWEEN THE LINES

A *theme* is a "message" found in a literary work. An *inference* is a conclusion drawn from facts. Analyze the story by choosing the best answer to each question below.

**1. A theme for this story is**

   Ⓐ séances are just a hoax.

   Ⓑ fear can make people do unusual, sometimes even bizarre, things.

   Ⓒ take time to appreciate your loved ones because you never know when you might lose them.

   Ⓓ guns are dangerous weapons.

**2. What conclusion about Sarah can you draw from paragraphs 4–5? Write your answer using complete sentences.**

_____

_____

_____

_____

_____

_____

**3. What conclusion can you draw from paragraphs 30–31?**

   Ⓐ Sarah had to get a job to pay for all those workers.

   Ⓑ Many workers weren't willing to work late-night shifts and holidays.

   Ⓒ Sarah's house used so many workers, other people weren't able to build homes.

   Ⓓ Over the years, Sarah's house provided work for many people.

**4. It can be inferred from the story that**

   Ⓐ Sarah's house must be quite an unusual sight today.

   Ⓑ Sarah was a friendly neighbor.

   Ⓒ building supplies were very cheap at that time.

   Ⓓ Sarah made lots of friends as she got older.

———■———

## DETERMINING CAUSE AND EFFECT

Choose the best answer for the following questions to show the relationship between *what* happened in the story (*effects*) and *why* those things happened (*causes*).

**1. Because of her family's deaths,**

Ⓐ Sarah became a medium.

Ⓑ the Winchesters adopted another baby.

Ⓒ Sarah withdrew from society.

Ⓓ Sarah and her husband moved to California.

**2. What happened because Sarah attended a séance?**

Ⓐ She became convinced that her family was cursed.

Ⓑ Her dead husband began to haunt her.

Ⓒ The Winchester company stopped making rifles.

Ⓓ She decided to sell the family business.

**3. Why did Sarah move to California?**

Ⓐ She believed her dead husband told her to.

Ⓑ She wanted to move the company to a warmer climate.

Ⓒ She knew people in California believed in séances.

Ⓓ She wanted to start her life over in a new place.

**4. Why did Sarah sleep in a different bedroom every night?**

Ⓐ She couldn't find a room that was comfortable.

Ⓑ She was afraid of earthquakes.

Ⓒ The sound of the builders kept her awake.

Ⓓ She was trying to hide from the ghosts.

———■———

# USING CONTEXT CLUES

Skilled readers can often find the meaning of unfamiliar words by using *context clues*. This means they study the way the words are used in the text. Use the context clues in the excerpts below to determine the meaning of the **bold-faced** words. Then choose the answer that best matches the meaning of the word.

**1.** "The **craze** was started in 1848 by a young woman named Margaret Fox and her two sisters."

*CLUE*: "Spiritualism had been very popular in America for about 40 years. . . . Many people were convinced that they were communicating with dead relatives and friends through the Fox sisters."

  Ⓐ fad

  Ⓑ party

  Ⓒ mystery

  Ⓓ story

**2.** "Did a curse seem that **far-fetched**?"

*CLUE*: "[Sarah] didn't want to believe what she had heard. But yet. . . . It did seem that her family had experienced its share of bad luck."

  Ⓐ true

  Ⓑ unlikely

  Ⓒ believable

  Ⓓ serious

**3.** "And each night, Sarah **emerged** from her hidden room with new plans for the next day's construction."

*CLUE*: "And she only entered her hidden séance room when she felt sure that the angry ghosts had lost her trail."

  Ⓐ came forth

  Ⓑ disappeared

  Ⓒ hid

  Ⓓ escaped

**4.** " [Sarah] often held **lavish** banquets for 12 guests, making a total of 13 at the table."

*CLUE*: "Although the food was real and quite excellent, Sarah was the only visible guest."

  Ⓐ stingy

  Ⓑ unattractive

  Ⓒ noisy

  Ⓓ fancy

# End-of-Unit Activities

1. This unit was titled "Ghosts Among the Living." What characteristic do ghost stories have in common? List 4 characteristics below. Then give at least one example from one of the stories to back up each of your choices. Stretch your thinking and avoid answers such as "They all involve a ghost."

**Characteristic 1** _____

Example: _____

_____

_____

**Characteristic 2** _____

Example: _____

_____

_____

**Characteristic 3** _____

Example: _____

_____

_____

**Characteristic 4** _____

Example: _____

_____

_____

# End-of-Unit Activities

**2. Rank each of the stories in this unit, from the one you liked the most to the one you liked the least. Then write a paragraph describing why you liked the story you ranked *1* the best.**

**LESSON 1** Ranking _____

_____

_____

_____

**LESSON 2** Ranking _____

_____

_____

_____

**LESSON 3** Ranking _____

_____

_____

_____

**LESSON 4** Ranking _____

_____

_____

_____

Why did you like the story you ranked *1* the best?

_____

_____

_____

# Words-Per-Minute Chart

## Directions:

Use the chart to find your words-per-minute reading speed. Refer to the reading time you recorded at the end of each story. Find your reading time in seconds along the left-hand side of the chart or minutes and seconds along the right-hand side of the chart. Your words-per-minute score will be listed next to the time in the column below the appropriate lesson number.

| No. of Words | Lesson 1 1,979 | Lesson 2 4,882 | Lesson 3 2,914 | Lesson 4 2,054 | Minutes and Seconds |
|---|---|---|---|---|---|
| 360 | 330 | 814 | 486 | 342 | 6:00 |
| 380 | 312 | 771 | 460 | 324 | 6:20 |
| 400 | 297 | 732 | 437 | 308 | 6:40 |
| 420 | 283 | 697 | 416 | 293 | 7:00 |
| 440 | 270 | 666 | 397 | 280 | 7:20 |
| 460 | 258 | 637 | 380 | 268 | 7:40 |
| 480 | 247 | 610 | 364 | 257 | 8:00 |
| 500 | 237 | 586 | 350 | 246 | 8:20 |
| 520 | 228 | 563 | 336 | 237 | 8:40 |
| 540 | 220 | 542 | 324 | 228 | 9:00 |
| 560 | 212 | 523 | 312 | 220 | 9:20 |
| 580 | 205 | 505 | 301 | 212 | 9:40 |
| 600 | 198 | 488 | 291 | 205 | 10:00 |
| 620 | 192 | 472 | 282 | 199 | 10:20 |
| 640 | 186 | 458 | 273 | 193 | 10:40 |
| 660 | 180 | 444 | 265 | 187 | 11:00 |
| 680 | 175 | 431 | 257 | 181 | 11:20 |
| 700 | 170 | 418 | 250 | 176 | 11:40 |
| 720 | 165 | 407 | 243 | 171 | 12:00 |
| 740 | 160 | 396 | 236 | 167 | 12:20 |
| 760 | 156 | 385 | 230 | 162 | 12:40 |
| 780 | 152 | 376 | 224 | 158 | 13:00 |
| 800 | 148 | 366 | 219 | 154 | 13:20 |
| 820 | 145 | 357 | 213 | 150 | 13:40 |
| 840 | 141 | 349 | 208 | 147 | 14:00 |
| 860 | 138 | 341 | 203 | 143 | 14:20 |
| 880 | 135 | 333 | 199 | 140 | 14:40 |
| 900 | 132 | 325 | 194 | 137 | 15:00 |
| 920 | 129 | 318 | 190 | 134 | 15:20 |
| 940 | 126 | 312 | 186 | 131 | 15:40 |
| 960 | 124 | 305 | 182 | 128 | 16:00 |
| 980 | 121 | 299 | 178 | 126 | 16:20 |
| 1,000 | 119 | 293 | 175 | 123 | 16:40 |
| 1,020 | 116 | 287 | 171 | 121 | 17:00 |
| 1,040 | 114 | 282 | 168 | 119 | 17:20 |
| 1,060 | 112 | 276 | 165 | 116 | 17:40 |
| 1,080 | 110 | 271 | 162 | 114 | 18:00 |
| 1,100 | 108 | 266 | 159 | 112 | 18:20 |
| 1,120 | 106 | 262 | 156 | 110 | 18:40 |
| 1,140 | 104 | 257 | 153 | 108 | 19:00 |
| 1,160 | 102 | 253 | 151 | 106 | 19:20 |
| 1,180 | 101 | 248 | 148 | 104 | 19:40 |
| 1,200 | 99 | 244 | 146 | 103 | 20:00 |
| 1,220 | 97 | 240 | 143 | 101 | 20:20 |
| 1,240 | 96 | 236 | 141 | 99 | 20:40 |
| 1,260 | 94 | 232 | 139 | 98 | 21:00 |
| 1,280 | 93 | 229 | 137 | 96 | 21:20 |
| 1,300 | 91 | 225 | 134 | 95 | 21:40 |
| 1,320 | 90 | 222 | 132 | 93 | 22:00 |
| 1,340 | 89 | 219 | 130 | 92 | 22:20 |
| 1,360 | 87 | 215 | 129 | 91 | 22:40 |
| 1,380 | 86 | 212 | 127 | 89 | 23:00 |
| 1,400 | 85 | 209 | 125 | 88 | 23:20 |
| 1,420 | 84 | 206 | 123 | 87 | 23:40 |
| 1,440 | 82 | 203 | 121 | 86 | 24:00 |

Seconds

# the dark side
# of human nature

**LESSON 5**

# A Game of Chess

Robert Barr

Here is a copy of the letter Henri Dumont wrote to his uncle, Count Ferrand, in Paris. It was written two days before Henri's death in Budapest, Hungary. It explains much about this story.

2*My Dear Uncle,*

*From my earlier letters, you know the government here is dishonest. I knew this before I left France. I was prepared to bribe officials. But it is much worse than I imagined.*

3*The worst is Schwikoff, editor of the* Gazette. *He told me his paper could ruin our chances to do business here. I believe that is true. I paid him large sums of money. Still, he asked for more.*

4*At last I got all the papers signed. We will be able to build our electrical plant here.*

5*I thought Schwikoff might be angry at the news. After all, there would be no reason to pay him any more bribes. But he surprised me.*

*When I saw him again, he was friendly. He even asked me to join him in a game of chess.*

6*We hadn't been playing for long when he suddenly said I had cheated. I tried to explain my move. However, he threw a glass of wine in my face. Then he challenged me to a duel.*

7*I have served as a soldier in the French Army. I could not ignore his insult—or his challenge. He is said to be skilled with a sword. And I am out of practice at swordplay. So I know that I shall probably die.*

8*At least I have done what you sent me here to do. Our company has the right to do business in Budapest.*

9*Schwikoff and I will meet about the time you get this letter. We fight at daybreak with swords.*

10*I send my love to you, dear uncle.*

*Your nephew,*

*Henri*

64

[11]The old man's hand shook as he put down the letter. He looked at the clock. It was late morning in Budapest. The duel would be over.

[12]Count Ferrand's family had lost its fortune during the French Revolution. But the count had turned to science. His ideas made a lot of money, and now he was a rich man. He ran one of the largest electric companies in Paris.

[13]No one in the company knew that Henri was the count's nephew. The count had believed the young man should learn the business by working his way up. He didn't want his nephew to receive special treatment.

[14]The count looked at the clock once more. There was nothing to do but wait for word about Henri. It was the plant manager who brought it to him.

[15]"I have some bad news, sir," said the manager. "The young man we sent to Budapest was killed this morning in a duel. He has no family here. I suppose he should be buried there."

[16]"Have his body brought back to France," the count said quietly.

[17]And it was done. Later, the old count surprised everyone. He said that he was going to go to Budapest.

*The old man's hand shook as he put down the letter.*

He would run the new plant himself.

[18]Once he arrived in Budapest, the count set to work. He wouldn't talk to anyone while the plant was being built. He concentrated only on his work. At last everything was done as he wanted.

[19]One of the first people the count saw in his private office was Schwikoff. The newspaper editor had asked for a meeting. He said he wanted to write a story about the new electrical plant.

[20]The old count greeted his visitor politely. He told Schwikoff that he was ready to tell him everything he needed to know.

[21] Schwikoff smiled. "To tell you the truth, sir, I didn't really come for a story," said the editor. "I thought we might make some kind of deal. It would be good for your company to have my paper on your side. I could make it much easier for you to do business here."

[22] "I won't pretend that I don't understand," said the count. "However, I was told that you had already been given a lot of money. And that any problems your paper could cause us had been taken care of."

[23] "The sums I received were small," said Schwikoff. "I hoped that once the plant was in business, you would be more generous."

[24] The count looked at some papers on his desk. "Am I right in saying that you were given more than 10,000 francs already?" he asked.

[25] "It may have been something like that," said Schwikoff. "I don't keep careful records of these matters."

[26] "It is a lot of money," said the count.

[27] "Yes, but you must remember what you got for it," said Schwikoff. "You can make money off every person in this city now."

[28] "Well, I am a businessman," said the count. "I like to know exactly what is going on. So I will ask you to name an amount that will end this matter."

[29] "I think 20,000 francs would do it," said Schwikoff.

[30] "That is a lot," said the count. "However, I will agree. If you take the money in payments of 1,000 francs a month."

[31] "That would take nearly two years!" said Schwikoff. "Life is short. Who knows what could happen in two years?"

[32] "Or even in a day," agreed the count. He paused; then he continued. "Still, we spent a lot of money to build this plant. And we are not making anything yet. I must insist on payments."

[33] "Fine," said Schwikoff at last. "As long as you make the first payment now."

[34] "I don't keep that much money here," said the count. "But if you come back tonight, I will have it."

[35] "Very well," said Schwikoff.

[36] "I want your visit to be a secret," added the count. "I don't want anyone else to expect this kind of money."

[37] "I understand," said Schwikoff.

[38]"Come here at 8:00," instructed the count. "Everyone else will be gone by then. I will leave the back door unlocked. Come here to my office, and I will have the money. Now, I must ask you to leave."

[39]At exactly 8:00, the office door opened and Schwikoff entered. "I hope I have not kept you waiting," he said.

[40]"No," said the count. "The money is upstairs. Please follow me."

[41]They climbed four sets of stairs. At last they came to a large, brightly lit room.

[42]"This is my laboratory," explained the count. "I do my electrical experiments here."

[43]It was a remarkable room. There were no windows. On one wall there were many switches of brass and copper and steel. About ten feet from the door, the wooden floor ended. Most of the rest of the room was laid out as a huge chessboard with squares of copper and steel.

[44]On the other side of the chessboard, there was more wooden flooring. A desk and some chairs sat there. On the desk was a pile of gold. Schwikoff's eyes glittered at the sight.

[45]Near the desk was a large open fireplace. Schwikoff had never seen one like it. In the center was what looked like a huge bathtub.

[46]The count noticed Schwikoff's interest. "That is my invention," he said. "An electric furnace. Probably the largest in the world."

[47]"I see," said Schwikoff. "And is this a chessboard on the floor?"

[48]"Yes, I love chess," answered the count.

[49]"So do I," replied Schwikoff.

[50]"Then we must have a game," said the count.

[51]"Where are your chessmen?" asked Schwikoff. "They must be huge."

[52]"This board is for living chessmen," said the count. "The squares are made of copper and steel. The black line around each square is hard rubber. That keeps the electricity from traveling from one square to another."

[53]"So you use electricity when playing?" asked Schwikoff.

[54]"Oh, electricity has something to do with the game," said the count. "I will explain it to you. But first, would you count the money?"

[55]The old man led the way across the chessboard. He offered a chair to

Schwikoff. The count carried the other chair over the chessboard. He put it down near the switches. Now the chessboard was between the two men.

[56] The count turned a knob. A bright flash lit the room. Schwikoff looked up, then went back to his counting. At last he said, "It is all here."

[57] "Please, don't leave your chair," ordered the count. "The chessboard is now a belt of death between us. The electricity is turned on. A man stepping anywhere on the board would be killed instantly."

[58] "Is this a joke?" asked Schwikoff. He was pale, and he didn't move from his chair.

[59] "It is not joke, as you will learn," said the count. "I will tell you all about it. All these knobs and switches let me control the board. Each one turns on a certain combination of squares."

[60] The count turned a few knobs. Steellike fire shot from some squares. "When I started talking, the whole board was electrified," the count said. "Now, it is not. A man could walk across. His chances of reaching this side alive are 3 to 1."

[61] Schwikoff jumped to his feet, ready to make a run for it. But the count turned more knobs.

[62] "If you start to run, I will turn on all the electricity," the count said. "You must keep a cool head on your shoulders, Mr. Schwikoff. Otherwise, you have no chance."

[63] Schwikoff took a gun from his coat pocket.

[64] The count went on talking. "You can easily shoot me dead. But I thought about that," he said. "I left a letter on my desk. It says that I went to Paris and will not be back for a month. It also says that no one is to enter this room while I am gone. The walls, ceilings, and floor are all soundproof. You could shout at the top of your lungs, and no one would hear you. The door is locked and there is no way out but the chimney. And if you look at that, you will see that it is now white-hot. There is no way out."

[65] Schwikoff sank back into his chair. "Why do you want to kill me?" he asked. "You can keep your money. I won't tell anyone what happened."

[66] "Oh, I don't care about the money," said the count.

[67] "Is it because I killed your employee?" asked Schwikoff.

[68] "He was my nephew," replied the count. "He was like a son to me.

Because of you, I am now a childless old man. My money means nothing to me. Now, are you ready to listen to the rules of the game?"

[69]"Yes," Schwikoff said after a pause.

[70]"First, throw your gun into the corner beside me," ordered the count.

[71]Schwikoff held the gun for a moment longer, then threw it across the metal floor.

[72]The old man turned another knob. "There, now you have a chance at life. Thirty-two of the squares are electrified. The other 32 are safe. Stand now on the square that belongs to the black king."

[73]"And die there," said Schwikoff.

[74]"No, that square is safe," said the count. "You are going to play the most important game of chess ever. The other player is death. You can move one square in any direction. That means you will always have eight squares to choose from. Most of the time, four squares will be safe. If you reach this side safely, you can go. But if you touch one of the electrified squares, you will die."

[75]"And you are in no danger. Is that fair?" asked Schwikoff.

[76]"As fair as it was for my nephew to duel with you," said the count. "He was not your match with swords. You knew that. However, we are not talking of his fate now. We are talking of yours. You have two minutes to stand on the king's square. If you don't move, I will turn on all the electricity and leave you here. With the electricity on full, the building will soon catch fire."

[77]Schwikoff stood still while the old man counted down the seconds. Finally, he stepped onto the king's square.

[78]"Good!" cried the count. "See, I told you it was safe. Now you have two minutes to move to another square."

[79]Schwikoff stepped onto another square. He stood there, breathing hard, but alive.

[80]"Two minutes to make the next move," repeated the count.

[81]"No!" shouted Schwikoff. "I moved right away last time. So I have four minutes now. I must keep cool. I must have control."

[82]However, by now, his voice was almost a scream. "I am calm!" he shouted. "But this isn't a game. It's murder!"

[83]"Take all the time you want then," said the count.

[84]Schwikoff stood there in

silence. But it was a silence broken now and then by the crackle of electricity. He looked fearfully at the squares. He thought more time would be to his advantage. But it only weakened his nerve.

[85]Then he balanced on his left foot. His right toe hung over one of the steel squares. Schwikoff felt a strange thrill pass through his body. At once, he snatched his foot back. He leaned back and forth, almost falling. He crouched down to save himself.

[86]"Mercy! Mercy!" he cried. "I have been punished enough."

[87]"Not so," said the count.

[88]Suddenly, Schwikoff jumped forward. He had lost all self-control. His eyes were wild. His outstretched hands reached for the polished metal. At once he stiffened and fell dead on the chessboard.

[89]There was no pity in the old count's eyes. He turned off the electricity. Then he rose and walked to the body. He turned it over with his foot. Then he removed one of Schwikoff's boots. He tore out a thin layer of cork.

[90]"Just as I thought," he said. "There was one thing I hadn't considered. I knew he was safe as soon as he stepped on the second square. It was electrified, yet nothing happened to him. With this cork in his boots, he could have walked across the board. If he had been a bit braver, he would have made it."

---

*If you have been timing your reading speed for this story, record your time below.*

_____ : _____

**Minutes**      **Seconds**

---

## UNDERSTANDING THE MAIN IDEA

The following questions will demonstrate your understanding of what the story is about, or the *main idea*. Choose the best answer for each question.

**1. This story is mainly about**

Ⓐ the history of chess.

Ⓑ an innovative electricity plant.

Ⓒ two men who compete in a world chess tournament.

Ⓓ a man who uses chess as a means of revenge.

**2. This story could have been titled**

Ⓐ "Chess Pieces and Their Significance."

Ⓑ "Checkmate with Death."

Ⓒ "A Shocking Source of Power."

Ⓓ "The Tournament of Champions."

**3. Which detail best supports the main idea of this story?**

Ⓐ Henri served as a soldier in the French Army.

Ⓑ Schwikoff asked the count for 20,000 francs.

Ⓒ Count Ferrand switched on the electricity to the chess board.

Ⓓ Near the count's desk was a large open fireplace.

**4. Find another detail that supports the main idea of this story. Write it on the lines below.**

_____

_____

_____

## RECALLING FACTS

The following questions will test how well you remember the facts in the story you just read. Choose the best answer for each question.

**1. Henri was Count Ferrand's**

Ⓐ son.

Ⓑ assistant.

Ⓒ chess partner.

Ⓓ nephew.

**2. Henri was killed in**

Ⓐ a duel.

Ⓑ an electrical accident.

Ⓒ Paris.

Ⓓ battle.

**3. From Count Ferrand, Schwikoff demanded**

Ⓐ an explanation.

Ⓑ work.

Ⓒ money.

Ⓓ a game of chess.

**4. Count Ferrand's huge chessboard used**

Ⓐ animals as the chess pieces.

Ⓑ electricity.

Ⓒ soldiers as the chess pieces.

Ⓓ cork as the base of the board.

## READING BETWEEN THE LINES

A *theme* is a "message" found in a literary work. An *inference* is a conclusion drawn from facts. Analyze the story by choosing the best answer to each question below.

**1. A theme for this story is**

Ⓐ chess is a dangerous game.

Ⓑ dueling is a fair way to settle an argument.

Ⓒ bribery is an acceptable practice.

Ⓓ impatience often leads to misfortune.

**2. What conclusion can you draw from paragraphs 2–7?**

Ⓐ Schwikoff generally liked Henri.

Ⓑ Schwikoff's accusation and challenge were planned.

Ⓒ Henri was not a very good soldier.

Ⓓ Schwikoff was an honest man trying to make an honest living.

**3. What conclusion can you draw from paragraphs 28–32?**

Ⓐ Count Ferrand was hinting that he was planning on killing Schwikoff.

Ⓑ Count Ferrand was broke.

Ⓒ Schwikoff was very generous at only asking for 20,000 francs.

Ⓓ Schwikoff was very patient.

**4. It can be inferred from the story that**

Ⓐ Count Ferrand felt bad about Schwikoff's death.

Ⓑ Henri was a coward.

Ⓒ the chessboard wasn't really charged with electricity.

Ⓓ Schwikoff's death didn't bother Count Ferrand.

## DETERMINING
## CAUSE AND EFFECT

Choose the best answer for the following questions to show the relationship between *what* happened in the story (*effects*) and *why* those things happened (*causes*).

**1. Because Henri was out of practice at swordplay,**

Ⓐ he died.

Ⓑ he demanded a week to practice before the duel.

Ⓒ he refused Schwikoff's challenge to a duel.

Ⓓ he became a soldier in the French Army.

**2. What happened because Count Ferrand went to Budapest to run the new electrical plant?**

Ⓐ Henri was killed.

Ⓑ Schwikoff visited with bribery threats.

Ⓒ His Paris plant went bankrupt.

Ⓓ He challenged Schwikoff to a duel with swords.

**3. Why did Count Ferrand say he wanted Schwikoff's visit to be a secret?**

Ⓐ He said he didn't want anyone else to expect money from him.

Ⓑ He said he didn't want anyone else to know about his huge chessboard.

Ⓒ He said he didn't want anyone to know about the electrical plant.

Ⓓ He said he didn't want people to know that he was friends with Schwikoff.

**4. Why could Schwikoff have survived the chess game if he were braver?**

_____

_____

_____

_____

_____

_____

## USING CONTEXT CLUES

Skilled readers can often find the meaning of unfamiliar words by using *context clues*. This means they study the way the words are used in the text. Use the context clues in the excerpts below to determine the meaning of the **bold-faced** words. Then chose the answer that best matches the meaning of the word.

**1.** "I was prepared to **bribe** officials."

*CLUE*: "[Schwikoff] told me his paper could ruin our chances to do business here. . . . I paid him large sums of money."

   Ⓐ meet

   Ⓑ reward

   Ⓒ pay off

   Ⓓ hire

**2.** "Count Ferrand's family had lost its **fortune** during the French Revolution."

*CLUE*: "[The count's] ideas made a lot of money, and now he was a rich man."

   Ⓐ wealth

   Ⓑ members

   Ⓒ luck

   Ⓓ prediction

**3.** "It was a **remarkable** room."

*CLUE*: "There were no windows. On one wall there were many switches of brass and steel. . . . Most of the rest of the room was laid out as a huge chessboard with squares of copper and steel."

   Ⓐ huge

   Ⓑ unusual

   Ⓒ ordinary

   Ⓓ conversational

**4.** " 'A man stepping anywhere on the board would be killed **instantly**.' "

*CLUE*: " 'The chessboard is now a belt of death between us. The electricity is turned on.' "

   Ⓐ eventually

   Ⓑ slowly

   Ⓒ neatly

   Ⓓ at once

# The Lalaurie House

Do you believe that a deed can be so evil that it poisons the place where it happened for years to come? Some people in New Orleans would answer "yes" to that question. They say that's why the Lalaurie house has been haunted for so long.

²The old mansion once hid a monstrous secret. Even later, those who went there sometimes encountered the horrors themselves. For example, in the 1830s an African American man was spending the night in the mansion. He awoke to find himself being choked by a pair of ghostly hands. Bending over him was the figure of a pale woman with dark hair.

³The woman had a firm grip on the man's throat, and her fury was so great that he could not break free. He was nearly unconscious—probably never to awaken again—when another pair of hands appeared. The hands of a black man pried the pale ones away from his throat. As the victim gasped for breath, the attacker and the rescuer grappled with each other. Still struggling, they faded from sight.

⁴The attacker was surely the spirit of Madame Delphine Lalaurie herself. It was she whose terrible deeds had poisoned the house and made it repulsive—even dangerous—to others.

⁵The records are unclear about just when the mansion was built. But by 1831, Madame Delphine Lalaurie had either inherited it from her second husband, bought it, or had it built herself. Her first two husbands had died. She lived in the mansion with her third husband, Dr. Leonard Louis Lalaurie.

⁶The three-story Lalaurie mansion had more than 40 rooms. It was designed and decorated to impress the highest social classes of New Orleans. Its many parlors and dining

rooms featured hand-carved doors, crystal chandeliers, and huge fireplaces. Madame Lalaurie filled the rooms with fine furniture and mirrors and paintings by well-known artists. She bought expensive gold and silver serving dishes and crystal glassware. She demanded elegant things that only great wealth could provide.

[7]Delphine Lalaurie gave splendid parties and soon gained a reputation as a charming hostess. She quickly rose to prominence in New Orleans society. She was said to be sweet and gracious and was even noted for her good deeds. And yet, there were ugly rumors . . .

[8]As in other rich families of the old South, the Lalauries' needs were taken care of by slaves. Perhaps the evil of slavery itself twisted Delphine Lalaurie's mind. Or perhaps she was just one of those soulless people who welcome the opportunity to mistreat others. In any case, it was becoming apparent that there were two sides to Madame Lalaurie.

[9]The neighbors and frequent guests began noticing that the Lalaurie slaves often seemed to disappear and were immediately replaced by others. If anyone asked, Madame Lalaurie explained that the missing slaves had been sold to other owners. Some, she said, had

merely vanished—doubtless runaways. But as time went by, rumors continued that she treated her slaves harshly. Although her

*Nightmares and Cold Sweats*

neighbors and friends began to be concerned, no one actually confronted her about the matter.

[10]Then one day, the mistress of the mansion was seen beating a child with a leather whip. She was a little slave girl—Delphine Lalaurie's personal maid. When the child turned and ran, the woman chased her, furiously waving her whip.

[11]In terror, the child fled into the house, up a winding stairway, and onto a balcony. When the angry mistress still followed, the child scrambled across the balcony railing. She ran blindly over the edge of the roof and fell to her death in the courtyard below.

[12]The dead child was quietly buried in an abandoned well at the rear of the house. Apparently, Madame Lalaurie wished to keep the matter a secret. But this time, a number of people had seen what happened. They finally took action. After all, there was a law that prohibited the cruel treatment of slaves. New Orleans authorities used that law to fine Madame Lalaurie and to take her slaves away from her.

[13]But the wealthy woman was more determined than the authorities. She talked some relatives into buying the slaves when they were sold at auction. Then she got the relatives to give her slaves back to her.

[14]Madame Lalaurie probably insisted that she couldn't bear to part with her dear servants. But more likely, it was just that they knew too much. She probably didn't want them talking to new owners. For some reason, the authorities didn't forbid her to have new slaves, or even to take the old ones back.

[15]It might have all ended there. The New Orleans legal system had done what it could. Madame Lalaurie would now be more careful about how she behaved, at least when anyone was watching.

[16]However, the truth about Delphine Lalaurie was finally revealed by the actions of an old slave woman. She was the cook in the mansion's kitchen. It was said that the old woman was often kept chained to the fireplace she used for cooking. She prepared fabulous dinners for the elegant guests upstairs, but her own life was made miserable by the mansion's owner.

[17]Apparently this old woman was unable to live with the mansion's secret horrors any longer. She decided to do something about it herself. On April 10, 1834, she set fire to the Lalaurie mansion.

[18]As the fire swept the mansion, New Orleans firefighters rushed to

put it out. Some remarked that there seemed to be very few slaves helping to carry out the Lalaurie's belongings. When they rescued the old woman from the kitchen, she begged them to open a door that led to an attic apartment.

[19]"Human beings are locked in up there!" the old woman cried.

[20]The firefighters rushed to free those who were trapped. However, neither the old woman's pleas nor the long-standing rumors prepared the men for what they found. It is said that one of them fainted at the sight.

[21]Inside the room, male and female slaves were chained to the wall. Around their necks were heavy iron collars, and their feet were shackled. Some were tied down on what appeared to be operating tables. Many of them were dead and several others died soon after they were rescued. Some of the living pleaded for death to free them from their misery.

[22]These wretched people had been tortured in the cruelest ways imaginable. Some had been sliced open, had parts of their bodies cut away or had limbs cut off. One had her mouth stuffed with filth, then sewed shut. Others had fingernails ripped out, eyes gouged out, or

mouths pinned shut. A stick stuck out of a hole that had been drilled in one dead man's head. Black ants feasted on honey that had been smeared all over some of the women.

[23]The firefighters managed to contain the blaze. It is believed that Madame Lalaurie was still in the mansion at that time. But she was keeping away from the public eye. Her attitude had always been that slaves were property, to be used and discarded as the owner wished. But even in the slaveholding South, this kind of inhumanity was both unusual and intolerable.

[24]The next day, the New Orleans newspaper reported on the scene the firefighters had found. White citizens began to gather at the Lalaurie mansion, demanding justice for the horrible deeds. By nightfall, the area around the mansion was filled with people who showed no sign of leaving. They seemed certain to storm the house.

[25]Suddenly, a carriage appeared at the mansion's door. Dressed in elegant traveling clothes, Madame Lalaurie dashed out and entered the carriage. As it began to move, the crowd, startled by the woman's audacity, regained their senses. However, their efforts to stop the

carriage failed. It raced away, and the murderess escaped.

[26]Many years would pass before anyone would be able to stay in the Lalaurie mansion. For a very long time, most were not even willing to walk past it at night.

[27]Over the years, various people have tried to live in it. Others have tried to use the handsome old building for businesses of one kind or another.

[28]In 1837, a new owner could not sleep because of the groans he heard all night long. He rented out some rooms, but every tenant soon left. Every other business also closed shortly after opening. It is said that the spirits of the Lalaurie house celebrated wildly each time some new enterprise failed.

[29]During the 1870s, the house was a public high school for girls. In the 1880s, it became a school of music and dancing. Both failed miserably.

[30]Then the mansion was turned into an apartment building. One of the tenants was mysteriously found dead, and most others quickly moved out. Too many had seen horribly tortured figures wandering through the hallways.

[31]In the early 20th century, the Lalaurie mansion was turned into a tenement. During that time, one resident reported seeing a man carrying his own head in one arm. Others saw a tall black man in chains or heard groans and screams.

[32]One woman who went to check on her sleeping baby found an elegantly dressed white woman leaning over the child. The mother screamed, and the ghost-woman vanished. Even the poorest tenants moved out of the Lalaurie mansion as soon as they could.

[33]In the 1930s, the old house was turned into a bar called the "Haunted Saloon." The owner knew about the building's past. In fact, he enjoyed keeping records of the old ghost stories. He also kept a list of the many strange things experienced by his patrons. Even so, the bar didn't last long, and the place was next turned into a furniture store.

[34]The owner of the furniture store was plagued by mysterious attacks on his merchandise. Over and over again, he found the furniture covered with a foul-smelling and dirty liquid. Determined to stop the vandals, the owner kept watch one night with his shotgun. All night he stayed awake, but he saw nothing unusual. However, the furniture was again ruined when morning came.

Shortly thereafter, he, too, got out of the place.

[35]It wasn't until the late 1960s that the Lalaurie mansion became comfortable to live in. It was restored by a new owner, who made the front into a living area and the back into five luxury apartments. Some still claim to experience paranormal activity, while others deny witnessing anything "ghostly." But can a place that once housed such evil ever really get rid of it?

---

*If you have been timing your reading speed for this story, record your time below.*

_____ : _____

**Minutes**    **Seconds**

---

*Nightmares and Cold Sweats*

## UNDERSTANDING THE MAIN IDEA

The following questions will demonstrate your understanding of what the story is about, or the *main idea*. Choose the best answer for each question.

**1. This story is mainly about**

   Ⓐ a mansion owned by a woman known for her kindness toward slaves.

   Ⓑ a mansion where slaves tortured their mistress.

   Ⓒ a mansion where a woman tortured her slaves.

   Ⓓ a haunted mansion that burned to the ground.

**2. This story could have been titled**

   Ⓐ "The Mansion That Turned to Ashes."

   Ⓑ "A Safe Haven for Slaves."

   Ⓒ "Abusing a Slave Mistress."

   Ⓓ "House of Horrors."

**3. Which detail best supports the main idea of this story?**

   Ⓐ The three-story Lalaurie mansion had more than 40 rooms.

   Ⓑ Inside the room, male and female slaves were chained to the wall.

   Ⓒ During the 1870s, the house was a public high school for girls.

   Ⓓ Madame Lalaurie demanded elegant things that only great wealth could provide.

**4. Find another detail that supports the main idea of this story. Write it on the line below.**

## RECALLING FACTS

The following questions will test how well you remember the facts in the story you just read. Choose the best answer for each question.

**1. Neighbors and frequent guests began noticing that the Lalaurie slaves**

   Ⓐ seemed to disappear and were immediately replaced.

   Ⓑ acted very lovingly toward Madame Lalaurie.

   Ⓒ were very well trained.

   Ⓓ acted extremely disrespectful toward everyone.

**2. Pretend that you are a neighbor of Madame Lalaurie and you witnessed the incident with Madame Lalaurie and her personal maid, the slave girl. On another sheet of paper, describe what you saw.**

**3. When the firefighters came to rescue the old woman in the kitchen, she begged them to**

   Ⓐ arrest Madame Lalaurie.

   Ⓑ leave her in the house.

   Ⓒ open a door that led to an attic apartment.

   Ⓓ investigate the cellar.

**4. The Lalaurie mansion has most recently been used as a**

   Ⓐ saloon.

   Ⓑ furniture store.

   Ⓒ school of music and dance.

   Ⓓ house with apartments.

A *theme* is a "message" found in a literary work. An *inference* is a conclusion drawn from facts. Analyze the story by choosing the best answer to each question below.

**1. A possible theme for this story is**

Ⓐ evil is a powerful force.

Ⓑ abolishing slavery was foolish.

Ⓒ not everyone deserves to be treated equally.

Ⓓ wealth is more important than humanity.

**2. What conclusion can you draw from paragraphs 6–7?**

Ⓐ Madame Lalaurie didn't care about what anyone thought of her.

Ⓑ Madame Lalaurie's social life was very important to her.

Ⓒ Madame Lalaurie believed in living a simple life.

Ⓓ The Lalaurie mansion was a dump compared to the other New Orleans mansions.

**3. What conclusion can you draw from paragraphs 13–15?**

Ⓐ Madame Lalaurie's relatives didn't think she should have her slaves back.

Ⓑ Slaves were treated as equal to whites.

Ⓒ Madame Lalaurie really did care about the well-being of her slaves.

Ⓓ Madame Lalaurie was smarter than the system.

**4. It can be inferred from the story that**

Ⓐ the tortured slaves were not able to rest in peace after their deaths.

Ⓑ all of the "ghost sightings" in the Lalaurie mansion were hoaxes.

Ⓒ Madame Lalaurie felt bad about what she had done.

Ⓓ Madame Lalaurie spent the rest of her life in prison.

## DETERMINING CAUSE AND EFFECT

Choose the best answer for the following questions to show the relationship between *what* happened in the story (*effects*) and *why* those things happened (*causes*).

**1. Because a number of people had seen what happened to Madame Lalaurie's personal maid, Madame Lalaurie**

Ⓐ began treating her slaves fairly.

Ⓑ was arrested for murder.

Ⓒ had her slaves taken away from her.

Ⓓ treated her slaves harshly.

**2. What happened because Madame Lalaurie was more determined than the authorities?**

Ⓐ She had relatives buy her slaves back for her.

Ⓑ She had relatives buy her new slaves.

Ⓒ She kidnapped her slaves and forced them to work for her again.

Ⓓ She broke out of jail.

**3. Why did the old cook set the mansion on fire?**

Ⓐ She accidentally did so when preparing a meal.

Ⓑ She was afraid of the ghosts in the house.

Ⓒ She was no longer able to live with the mansion's secret horrors.

Ⓓ She wanted to die.

**4. Why did white citizens gather at the Lalaurie mansion after a newspaper reported on the scene the firefighters had found?**

Ⓐ They went to show their support for Madame Lalaurie.

Ⓑ They went to demand justice for the horrible deeds.

Ⓒ They didn't believe the newspapers.

Ⓓ They were all after a reward for the capture of Madame Lalaurie.

# USING CONTEXT CLUES

Skilled readers can often find the meaning of unfamiliar words by using *context clues*. This means they study the way the words are used in the text. Use the context clues in the excerpts below to determine the meaning of the **bold-faced** words. Then chose the answer that best matches the meaning of the word.

**1.** "She quickly rose to **prominence** in New Orleans society."

*CLUE*: "Delphine Lalaurie gave splendid parties and soon gained a reputation as a charming hostess."

   Ⓐ poverty

   Ⓑ popularity

   Ⓒ anger

   Ⓓ anonymity

**2.** "These **wretched** people had been tortured in the cruelest ways imaginable."

*CLUE*: "Some had been sliced open, had parts of their bodies cut away or had limbs cut off."

   Ⓐ lucky

   Ⓑ wicked

   Ⓒ deserving

   Ⓓ unfortunate

**3.** "As [the carriage] began to move, the crowd, startled by the woman's **audacity**, regained their senses."

*CLUE*: "Dressed in elegant clothes, Madame Lalaurie dashed out and entered the carriage . . . . It raced away, and the murderess escaped."

   Ⓐ boldness

   Ⓑ sadness

   Ⓒ shyness

   Ⓓ alarm

**4.** "The owner of the furniture store was **plagued** by mysterious attacks on his merchandise."

*CLUE*: "Determined to stop the vandals, the owner kept watch one night with his shotgun."

   Ⓐ diseased

   Ⓑ bothered

   Ⓒ pleased

   Ⓓ killed

*Nightmares and Cold Sweats*

# Sredni Vashtar

Saki

Conradin was ten years old. The doctor had given his professional opinion that the boy would not live another five years. The doctor was of weak character and counted for little. But Mrs. De Ropp agreed with him completely. And she counted for nearly everything.

[2] Mrs. De Ropp was Conradin's cousin and guardian. In his eyes, she represented three-fifths of the world's people—the three-fifths that were necessary and disagreeable and real. Conradin belonged to the other two-fifths—the two-fifths that were always fighting against the first. He kept that part deep inside his imagination.

[3] One of these days, Conradin supposed, he would give in to Mrs. De Ropp's powerful pressures. He would become weary and accept her tiresome diagnosis of his illness, her strict rules, and her drawn-out dullness. Without his imagination, he would have given in long ago. His thoughts went wild under the spur of his loneliness.

[4] Mrs. De Ropp would never have admitted to herself that she disliked Conradin. Not even in her most honest moments would she do that. She always defeated his wishes "for his good."

[5] Conradin hated her fiercely, but he was perfectly able to mask it. The few pleasures he could invent for himself gave him great joy. His happiness grew whenever it seemed likely that his invented pleasures would displease his guardian, who was completely locked out of his imagined world.

[6] Conradin found little to attract him in the dull, cheerless garden. Too many windows overlooked it— windows that were always ready to open with a message not to do this or that.

[7]The few fruit trees in the garden were set carefully out of his reach. The blooms seemed to be rare examples of their kind in this arid waste. No market-gardener would have offered ten shillings for their entire yearly crop.

[8]In a forgotten corner of the garden, however, was an unused toolshed of decent size. It was almost hidden behind a dismal bush. Conradin found a haven within its walls. To him, the toolshed could be a playroom or a cathedral.

[9]He had populated the toolshed with many familiar phantoms. He called them forth, partly from history and partly from his own brain. But the shed also boasted two inmates of flesh and blood. In one corner lived a ragged-feathered Houdan hen. The boy heaped affection on the hen, for his feelings had hardly any other outlet.

[10]Further back in the gloom stood a large cage. It was divided into sections. One of the sections was fronted with iron bars close together. This was the home of a large ferret. A friendly butcher boy had once smuggled it, cage and all, into the toolshed. Conradin had bought it in exchange for a long-hidden hoard of small silver.

[11]Conradin was dreadfully afraid of the graceful, sharp-fanged beast. But it was his most treasured possession. Its very presence in the toolshed was a secret joy. He carefully kept it from the knowledge of the Woman. (That was what he privately called his cousin.)

[12]And one day he created a wonderful name for the beast. He called it Sredni Vashtar. Heaven knows how he came up with this name. But from that moment, the ferret grew into a god and a religion.

[13]The Woman exercised her religion once a week at a nearby church. She took Conradin with her. But to him, the church service was like a strange rite.

[14]Every Thursday Conradin went into the dim, musty silence of the toolshed. There he worshipped before the wooden cage where Sredni Vashtar lived. The boy held mystical and complicated rites for the great ferret. When in season, red flowers were offered at the ferret's shrine. Scarlet berries were offered in the wintertime. For Sredni Vashtar was a god. And this god laid special importance on the fierce, impatient side of things. This was unlike the Woman's religion. As far as Conradin could see, hers went to great lengths in the other direction.

[15]During great festivals,

powdered nutmeg was scattered in front of the ferret's cage. It was essential to the offering that the nutmeg be stolen. These festivals occurred from time to time and were usually devoted to some passing occasion.

[16]On one such occasion, Mrs. De Ropp suffered from a sharp toothache for three days. Conradin kept up the festival during the entire three days. He almost managed to persuade himself that Sredni Vashtar had caused the toothache. If the pain had lasted for another day, the nutmeg supply would have been used up.

[17]The Houdan hen was never drawn into the cult of Sredni Vashtar. Conradin had long ago decided that she was an Anabaptist. He did not pretend to have the least knowledge as to what an Anabaptist was. But he privately hoped that it was daring and not very respectable. Mrs. De Ropp was the model on which he based his view of respectability. And Conradin hated all respectability.

[18]After a while, Conradin's interest in the toolshed began to attract his guardian's notice.

[19]"It is not good for him to be fooling around down there in all weather," she quickly decided.

[20]At breakfast one morning, she announced that the Houdan hen had been sold. It had been taken away overnight. She peered at Conradin with her shortsighted eyes. She was hoping for an outbreak of rage and sorrow. She was even ready to scold him with a flow of excellent lessons and reasoning.

[21]But Conradin said nothing. There was nothing to be said. Something perhaps in his determined face gave her a moment of uncertainty.

[22]At tea that afternoon, there was toast on the table. It was a treat that she usually banned. She claimed that it was bad for him and that the making of it "gave trouble." That was a deadly misdeed in her middle-class feminine eye.

[23]She saw that he did not touch it.

[24]"I thought you liked toast!" she exclaimed with a hurt look.

[25]"Sometimes," said Conradin.

[26]In the shed that evening, there was a change in the worship of the cage-god. Conradin usually chanted his praises. Tonight he asked a favor.

[27]"Do one thing for me, Sredni Vashtar."

[28]The thing was not named. Since Sredni Vashtar was a god, surely he

*Every evening Conradin prayed to Sredni Vashtar.*

was supposed to know what Conradin wished for. Conradin choked back a sob as he looked at that other empty corner. Then he went back to the world he so hated. And every night, in the welcome darkness of his bedroom, Conradin's bitter prayer went up. And every evening, in the dusk of the toolshed, he prayed again.

[29]"Do one thing for me, Sredni Vashtar."

[30]Mrs. De Ropp noticed that the visits to the shed did not stop. So one day, she went to the shed herself.

[31]"What are you keeping in that locked cage?" she asked. "I bet it's guinea pigs. I'll have them all cleared away."

[32]Conradin shut his lips tight. But the Woman searched his bedroom until she found the hidden key. Then she marched down to the shed to complete her discovery.

[33]It was a cold afternoon, and Conradin had been ordered to stay in the house. He stationed himself at the far window of the dining room. From there, the door of the shed could just be seen beyond the corner of the shrubbery.

*Nightmares and Cold Sweats*

[34]He saw the Woman enter. He imagined her opening the door of the sacred cage. She was peering down with her shortsighted eyes into the thick straw bed where his god lay hidden. Perhaps she would poke at the straw in her clumsy impatience.

[35]Conradin passionately breathed his prayer for the last time. But as he prayed, he knew that he did not believe. He knew that the Woman would soon come out with that pinched smile on her face—the very smile he hated so much. Then, in an hour or two, the gardener would carry away his wonderful god. It would no longer be a god. It would simply be a brown ferret in a cage.

[36]He knew that the Woman would triumph now as she always triumphed. He knew that he would grow ever more sickly under her pestering. He would grow weaker under her greater and more powerful wisdom. Then one day, nothing would matter much with him. And the doctor would be proved right.

[37]Conradin felt the sting and misery of his defeat. He began to chant the hymn of his threatened idol loudly and defiantly:

[38]*Sredni Vashtar went forth.*

*His thoughts were red thoughts,*
*and his teeth were white.*
*His enemies called for peace,*
*but he brought them death.*
*Sredni Vashtar the Beautiful.*

[39]Suddenly, he stopped his chanting. He drew closer to the window. The door of the shed still stood ajar. The minutes slipped by. They were long minutes.

[40]He watched the starlings running and flying in little groups across the lawn. He counted them over and over again. But he kept one eye on the swinging door.

[41]A sour-faced maid came in to lay the table for tea while Conradin stood and waited and watched. Hope crept by inches into his heart. Now a look of triumph began to blaze in his eyes. Before now, those eyes had only known the sad patience of defeat.

[42]Under his breath, he resumed the chant of victory and destruction. He sang it with a secret joy. And soon his eyes were rewarded.

[43]Out through that doorway came a long, low, yellow-and-brown beast. Its eyes were a-blink at the fading daylight. The fur of its jaws and throat was covered with a dark, wet stain. Conradin dropped to his knees.

[44]The great ferret made its way to a small brook at the foot of the garden. It drank for a moment. Then it crossed a little plank bridge and was lost to sight in the bushes. Such was the passing of Sredni Vashtar.

[45]"Tea is ready," said the sour-faced maid. "Where is the mistress?"

[46]"She went down to the shed some time ago," said Conradin.

[47]The maid went to summon her mistress to tea. While she did, Conradin fished a toasting fork out of the drawer. He began to toast himself a piece of bread. While the bread toasted, Conradin listened. He buttered his toast with much butter. And during the slow enjoyment of eating it, he listened again.

[48]Noises and silences came in quick spasms beyond the dining room door. He heard the loud, foolish screaming of the maid. Cries from the kitchen area answered. Then came scrambling footsteps. Someone was hastily sent for outside help.

[49]After a lull, there were frightened sobs. Then there was the shuffling tread of those who bore a heavy weight into the house.

[50]"Whoever will break it to the poor child? I couldn't for the life of me!" cried a shrill voice.

[51]While the others argued the matter among themselves, Conradin made himself another piece of toast.

---

*If you have been timing your reading speed for this story, record your time below.*

_____ : _____

*Minutes*     *Seconds*

---

*Nightmares and Cold Sweats*

## UNDERSTANDING THE MAIN IDEA

The following questions will demonstrate your understanding of what the story is about, or the *main idea*. Choose the best answer for each question.

**1. This story is mainly about**

ⓐ a boy who created his own dream world because his real life was miserable.

ⓑ the care and feeding of ferrets.

ⓒ the beliefs of the Anabaptists.

ⓓ a forgotten garden overrun with weeds.

**2. This story could have been titled**

ⓐ "Anabaptists and Other Religions."

ⓑ "A Secret God."

ⓒ "The Boy Who Loved Ferrets."

ⓓ "A Loving Guardian."

**3. Which detail best supports the main idea of the story?**

ⓐ Every Thursday, Conradin worshipped before the wooden cage where Sredni Vashtar lived.

ⓑ The doctor said Conradin would not live another five years.

ⓒ Conradin bought the ferret in exchange for some small silver.

ⓓ Conradin liked toast.

**4. Find another detail that supports the main idea of this story. Write it on the lines below.**

_____

_____

_____

## RECALLING FACTS

The following questions will test how well you remember the facts in the story you just read. Choose the best answer for each question.

**1. Mrs. De Ropp was Conradin's**

ⓐ teacher.

ⓑ guardian.

ⓒ mother.

ⓓ Houdan hen.

**2. Conradin's favorite place to escape Mrs. De Ropp was**

ⓐ the toolshed.

ⓑ his bedroom.

ⓒ the kitchen.

ⓓ the basement.

**3. To Conradin, Sredni Vashtar grew into**

ⓐ an enemy.

ⓑ a pet and a playmate.

ⓒ a god and a religion.

ⓓ a fierce protector.

**4. Sredni Vashtar shared the toolshed with**

ⓐ a Houdan hen.

ⓑ a black cat.

ⓒ a parakeet.

ⓓ Conradin's toys.

## READING BETWEEN THE LINES

A *theme* is a "message" found in a literary work. An *inference* is a conclusion drawn from facts. Analyze the story by choosing the best answer to each question below.

**1. A theme for this story is**

  Ⓐ ferrets don't make good pets.

  Ⓑ sometimes life isn't fair.

  Ⓒ religion often helps people through difficult times.

  Ⓓ people sometimes suffer for the cruel things they do.

**2. What conclusion can you draw from paragraphs 3–4?**

  Ⓐ Mrs. De Ropp adored Conradin.

  Ⓑ Mrs. De Ropp's house was a happy place to live.

  Ⓒ Mrs. De Ropp hated Conradin.

  Ⓓ Mrs. De Ropp had a kind, generous nature.

**3. What conclusion can you draw from paragraph 20?**

  Ⓐ Mrs. De Ropp enjoyed being cruel to Conradin.

  Ⓑ Breakfast is the best time to announce bad news.

  Ⓒ Mrs. De Ropp felt bad about getting rid of Conradin's hen.

  Ⓓ Mrs. De Ropp was blind.

**4. It can be inferred from the story that**

  Ⓐ Conradin taught Mrs. De Ropp how to worship Sredni Vashtar.

  Ⓑ Mrs. De Ropp decided to let Conradin bring the ferret's cage inside.

  Ⓒ Mrs. De Ropp and Conradin eventually became friends.

  Ⓓ the ferret killed Mrs. De Ropp.

## DETERMINING CAUSE AND EFFECT

Choose the best answer for the following questions to show the relationship between *what* happened in the story (*effects*) and *why* those things happened (*causes*).

**1. Because Mrs. De Ropp seemed to take pleasure in taking away the things he enjoyed, Conradin**

Ⓐ loved her.

Ⓑ was grateful to her.

Ⓒ admired her.

Ⓓ hated her.

**2. What happened because Conradin bought a ferret from a butcher boy?**

Ⓐ He spent most of his time alone in the toolshed, worshipping the ferret.

Ⓑ His health started to decline.

Ⓒ He became a happy, contented little boy.

Ⓓ He became more sure of himself and started making friends.

**3. Why did Conradin ask Sredni Vashtar for a favor?**

Ⓐ He could tell that he was getting sicker and sicker.

Ⓑ He was afraid Mrs. De Ropp was going to take the ferret away soon.

Ⓒ He wanted to surprise Mrs. De Ropp.

Ⓓ He wanted to find more nutmeg for his religious festivals.

**4. Why did Conradin's eyes blaze with triumph?**

Ⓐ He had just finished a long worship session.

Ⓑ He was told that he would soon move to a new home.

Ⓒ Mrs. De Ropp had been in the toolshed for a very long time.

Ⓓ Mrs. De Ropp allowed him to keep the ferret.

———— ▬ ————

## USING CONTEXT CLUES

Skilled readers can often find the meaning of unfamiliar words by using *context clues*. This means they study the way the words are used in the text. Use the context clues in the excerpts below to determine the meaning of the **bold-faced** words. Then choose the answer that best matches the meaning of the word.

**1.** "Conradin found a **haven** within its walls."

*CLUE*: "It was almost hidden behind a dismal bush. . . . To him, the toolshed could be a playroom or a cathedral."

   Ⓐ classroom

   Ⓑ hideaway

   Ⓒ library

   Ⓓ laboratory

**2.** "But [Conradin] privately hoped that it was daring and not very **respectable**." (paragraph 17)

Write what you think the **bold-faced** word means. Then record the context clues that led you to this definition.

Meaning:

_____

_____

_____

Context Clues:

_____

_____

_____

**3.** "[Conradin] **stationed** himself at the far window of the dining room."

*CLUE*: "From there, the door of the shed could be seen just beyond the corner of the shrubbery."

   Ⓐ discovered

   Ⓑ found

   Ⓒ positioned

   Ⓓ saw

**4.** " [Conradin] knew that the Woman would **triumph** now as she always triumphed."

*CLUE*: "He knew that the Woman would soon come out with that pinched smile on her face—the very smile he hated so much. Then, in an hour or two, the gardener would carry away his wonderful god."

   Ⓐ win

   Ⓑ challenge

   Ⓒ lose

   Ⓓ lie

# The Cask of Amontillado

### Edgar Allan Poe

Over the years, I had stood the thousand wrongs of Fortunato as best I could. But when he insulted me, I vowed revenge. However, you know the nature of my soul well. You will know that I never uttered a threat. Sooner or later, I would be avenged—this was a point definitely settled. But the very certainty with which it was decided ruled out the idea of risk.

[2] I must not only punish, but punish without being punished myself. A wrong is not paid back when retribution overtakes its avenger. It is also unpaid when the avenger fails to make himself known to him who has done the wrong.

[3] It must be understood that neither by word nor deed had I given myself away. Fortunato had no cause to doubt my goodwill. I continued, as usual, to smile in his face. He did not see that my smile now was at the thought of his destruction.

[4] He had a weak point—this Fortunato—although in other ways, he was a man to be respected and even feared. He prided himself on being an expert in wine. Few Italians have the true spirit of genius at this. For the most part, their enjoyment of wine is merely suited to the time and opportunity. Their purpose is to trick British and Austrian millionaires.

[5] In paintings and the study of gems, Fortunato, like his countrymen, was a quack. But in the matter of old wines, he was the real thing. And in this way, I did not differ from him very much. I knew about Italian wines myself and bought them whenever I could.

[6] It was about dusk one evening during the greatest madness of Carnival. I met my friend. He approached me with excessive

warmth, for he had been drinking much.

[7]The man wore the costume of a jester. He had on a tight-fitting striped dress. On top of his head was a pointed cap and bells. I was so pleased to see him that I thought I should never finish wringing his hand.

[8]I said to him, "My dear Fortunato, I'm so lucky to meet you! How remarkably well you look today! I have received a cask of what passes for Amontillado. And I have my doubts about whether it truly is Amontillado or not."

[9]"How?" asked Fortunato. "Amontillado? A cask? Impossible! And in the middle of Carnival!"

[10]"As I said, I have my doubts," I replied. "And I was silly enough to pay the full Amontillado price without consulting you. You were not to be found, and I was fearful of losing a bargain."

[11]"Amontillado!" Fortunato exclaimed.

[12]"I have my doubts," I replied.

[13]"Amontillado!" he repeated.

[14]"And I must satisfy them," I said.

[15]"Amontillado!"

[16]"Since you are busy, I am on my way to see Luchesi," I said. "If anyone knows his wines, it is he. He will tell me—"

[17]"Luchesi cannot tell Amontillado from Sherry," Fortunato interrupted.

[18]"And yet some fools would say that his taste is a match for your own," I challenged.

[19]"Come, let us go," he said.

[20]"Where?" I asked.

[21]"To your vaults," Fortunato answered.

[22]"My friend, no. I will not impose upon your good nature. I know you are on your way to meet someone. Luchesi—"

[23]"I am meeting no one. Come," Fortunato once again interrupted.

[24]"My friend, no. It is not that. But I see that you are suffering in the severe cold. The vaults are unbearably damp," I cautioned. "They are encrusted with nitre."

[25]"Let us go, nevertheless," Fortunato said. "The cold is nothing. Amontillado!"

[26]Thus speaking, Fortunato took my arm. I put on a mask of black silk and drew a cloak close around me. He hurried me to my home.

[27]There were no servants at home. They had run away to make merry in honor of the holiday. I had

told them that I should not return until the morning. And I had given them explicit orders not to stir from the house. These orders were enough, I knew, to ensure their disappearance. They were gone, one and all, as soon as my back was turned.

[28]I took two torches from their holders and gave one to Fortunato. I guided him through several groups of rooms to the archway that led to the vault. I passed down a long and winding staircase, warning him to be careful as he followed. We finally came to the bottom of our climb. We stood together on the damp ground of the catacombs that belonged to my family, the Montresors.

[29]My friend's step was unsteady, and the bells upon his cap jingled as he walked.

[30]"The cask?" he asked.

[31]"It is farther on," I said. "But see the white webwork that gleams from these cavern walls."

[32]He turned toward me and looked into my eyes. His misty eyes dribbled the tears of intoxication.

[33]"Nitre?" he asked, at length.

[34]"Nitre," I replied. "How long have you had that cough?"

[35]"Ugh! ugh! ugh!—ugh! ugh! ugh!—ugh! ugh! ugh!—ugh! ugh!

*Montresor led Fortunato down a long and winding staircase.*

ugh!—ugh! ugh! ugh!"

[36]My poor friend found it impossible to reply for many minutes.

[37]"It is nothing," he said at last.

[38]"Come," I said with decision. "We will go back. Your health is precious. You are rich, respected, admired, beloved. You are happy, as I once was. You are a man to be missed. For me it is no matter. We will go back. You will be ill, and I

cannot be to blame. Besides, there is Luchesi—"

[39]"Enough," he said. "The cough is nothing. It will not kill me. I shall not die of a cough."

[40]"True—true," I replied. "And indeed I did not mean to alarm you unnecessarily. But you should use proper caution. A drink of this Medoc will defend us from the damps."

[41]At this point, I drew a bottle from a long row of its fellows. I knocked off the neck of the bottle.

[42]"Drink," I said, giving him the wine.

[43]He raised it to his lips with a leer. He paused and nodded to me in a familiar way while his bells jingled.

[44]"I drink," he said, "to the buried that rest around us."

[45]"And I drink to your long life," I replied.

[46]He took my arm again, and we went on.

[47]"These vaults are very large," he noticed.

[48]"The Montresors were a great and large family."

[49]"I forget your coat of arms," he said.

[50]"A huge human foot of gold on a field of blue. The foot crushes a raging serpent, whose fangs are imbedded in the heel," I described.

[51]"And your motto?"

[52]"No one insults me without punishment."

[53]"Good!" he said.

[54]The wine sparkled in his eyes, and the bells jingled on his head. My own imagination grew warm with the Medoc. We had passed through walls of piled bones mixed with large and small casks. We reached the inner recesses of the catacombs.

[55]"The nitre!" I said. "See, it increases. It hangs like moss upon the vaults. We are below the river's bed. The drops of moisture trickle among the bones. Come, we will go back before it is too late. Your cough—"

[56]"It is nothing," he insisted. "Let us go on. But first, another drink of the Medoc."

[57]I broke a bottle of de Grâve and handed it to him. He emptied it at a breath. His eyes flashed with a fierce light. He laughed and threw the bottle upward with a motion I did not understand.

[58]I looked at him in surprise. He repeated the movement—a grotesque one.

[59]"You do not understand?" he said.

[60]"Not I," I replied.

[61]"Then you are not of the brotherhood," he said.

[62]"What do you mean?" I asked.

[63]"You are not of the Masons."

[64]"Oh yes, yes," I said. "Yes, yes."

[65]"You? Impossible! A Mason?"

[66]"A Mason," I replied.

[67]"A sign," he said.

[68]"It is this," I answered. I produced a trowel from beneath the folds of my cloak.

[69]"You jest!" he exclaimed, recoiling a few paces. "But let us go on to the Amontillado."

[70]"Be it so," I said, replacing the tool beneath my cloak. I offered him my arm, and he leaned upon it heavily. We continued on our way in search of the Amontillado. We passed through a range of low arches. We descended, walked a ways, and descended again, arriving at a deep crypt. Here the foulness of the air caused our torches to glow rather than flame.

[71]At the far end of the crypt was another smaller one. Its walls had been lined with human remains. They were piled up to the vault overhead in the style of the great catacombs of Paris. Three sides of this interior crypt were still decorated in this manner. From the fourth side, the bones had been thrown down. The bones lay scattered upon the earth, forming a mound of some size.

[72]A wall was exposed by the removal of the bones. Inside it, we saw still another space. It was about four feet deep, three wide, and six or seven high. It seemed to have been built for no special use. It was merely the space between two of the huge supports of the roof. It was backed by a wall of solid granite.

[73]Fortunato lifted up his dull torch. But it was in vain that he tried to see into the depths of the recess. The feeble light did not let us see its end.

[74]"Go on," I said. "In here is the Amontillado. As for Luchesi—"

[75]"He is an ignoramus," interrupted my friend. He stepped unsteadily forward. I followed right at his heels. He had reached the end of the space in an instant. Finding his progress stopped by the rock, he stood, stupidly confused.

[76]A moment more, and I had chained him to the granite. In its surface were two iron staples. They were about two feet apart from each other. From one of these staples hung a short chain; from the other hung a padlock. I threw the links

about his waist. It took but a few seconds to fasten it. He was much too shocked to resist. Withdrawing the key, I stepped back from the recess.

[77]"Pass your hand over the wall," I said. "You cannot help feeling the nitre. Indeed it is very damp. Once more let me beg you to return. No? Then I shall certainly leave you. But I must first do what little I can to make you feel at home."

[78]"The Amontillado!" cried my friend. He had not yet recovered from his shock.

[79]"True," I replied. "The Amontillado."

[80]As I said these words, I busied myself. I dug among the pile of bones. Throwing them aside, I soon uncovered a supply of building stone and mortar. I made use of these materials and my trowel. I began to vigorously wall up the entrance of the space.

[81]I had hardly laid the first row of masonry when I discovered that Fortunato's intoxication had mostly worn off. The earliest sign was a low moaning cry from the depths of the recess. It was not the cry of a drunken man.

[82]Then there was a long and stubborn silence. I laid the second row, and the third, and the fourth.

Then I heard the furious shaking of the chain. The noise lasted for several minutes. To listen to it with more enjoyment, I stopped my work and sat down upon the bones.

[83]When at last the clanking stopped, I took up my trowel again. I finished the fifth, the sixth, and the seventh rows without interruption. The wall was now nearly level with my chest. I again paused and held the torch over the mason work. It threw a few feeble rays upon the figure within.

[84]Suddenly a series of loud and shrill screams burst from the throat of the chained form. They drove me back violently. For a brief moment, I hesitated—I trembled.

[85]Unsheathing my sword, I began to grope with it about the recess. But a moment's thought reassured me. I placed my hand upon the solid material of the catacombs and felt satisfied. I went back to the wall. I replied to the yells of him who cried out. I echoed—I aided—I surpassed them in volume and in strength. I did this, and the caller grew still.

[86]It was not yet midnight, and my task was drawing to a close. I had completed the eighth, the ninth, and the tenth levels. I had finished a part of the eleventh—the last. There

remained but a single stone to be fitted and plastered in. I struggled with its weight. I put it partway in its intended place.

[87]But now there came from out of the space a low laugh. It made the hairs on my head stand up. It was followed by a sad voice, one that I had difficulty recognizing as that of the noble Fortunato.

[88]The voice said, "Ha! ha! ha!— hee! hee!—a very good joke indeed. An excellent jest. We will have many a rich laugh about it at the palazzo. Ho! ho! ho!—over our wine—ha! ha! ha!"

[89]"The Amontillado!" I said.

[90]"Hee! hee! hee!—hee! hee! hee!—yes, the Amontillado. But is it not getting late? Will not they be awaiting us at the palazzo, the Lady Fortunato and the rest? Let us be gone."

[91]"Yes," I said, "let us be gone."

[92]"For the love of God, Montresor!"

[93]"Yes," I said, "for the love of God!"

[94]But to these words I listened in vain for a reply. I grew impatient. I called aloud.

[95]"Fortunato!"

[96]No answer. I called again.

[97]"Fortunato!"

[98]No answer still. I thrust a torch through the remaining opening and let it fall within. Only a jingling of the bells came forth in reply. My heart grew sick—because of the dampness of the catacombs, of course.

[99]I hurried to end my work. I forced the last stone into its position. I plastered it up. Against the new masonry, I replaced the old wall of bones. And for half of a century, no mortal has disturbed them.

[100]May he rest in peace!

---

*If you have been timing your reading speed for this story, record your time below.*

_____ : _____

**Minutes**     **Seconds**

---

## UNDERSTANDING THE MAIN IDEA

The following questions will demonstrate your understanding of what the story is about, or the *main idea*. Choose the best answer for each question.

**1. This story is mainly about**

Ⓐ fine Spanish and Italian wines.

Ⓑ how the Montresor family buried their dead relatives.

Ⓒ a man who wanted to reward someone for helping him.

Ⓓ a man who wanted to get revenge.

**2. This story could have been titled**

Ⓐ "One Man's Revenge."

Ⓑ "Wines from Around the World."

Ⓒ "The Finest Reward."

Ⓓ "How to Store Wine."

**3. Which detail best supports the main idea of the story?**

Ⓐ Montresor got a great bargain on a cask of Amontillado.

Ⓑ Fortunato knew more about wine than Luchesi.

Ⓒ Fortunato knew a lot about Italian art.

Ⓓ Montresor tricked Fortunato into entering his vaults.

**4. Find another detail that supports the main idea of this story. Write it on the lines below.**

_____

_____

_____

## RECALLING FACTS

The following questions will test how well you remember the facts in the story you just read. Choose the best answer for each question.

**1. Fortunato prided himself on**

Ⓐ being a wine expert.

Ⓑ being a skilled court jester.

Ⓒ his artistic talents.

Ⓓ his ability to make friends.

**2. Monstresor's home was empty because**

Ⓐ no one wanted to see Montresor get his revenge.

Ⓑ everyone was out shopping for his or her own cask of Amontillado.

Ⓒ everyone was out celebrating the holiday.

Ⓓ they heard Fortunato was coming over.

**3. In the catacombs, the nitre on the walls**

Ⓐ smelled like sour wine.

Ⓑ made Montresor angry.

Ⓒ was a sign fine wine was stored there.

Ⓓ made Fortunato cough.

**4. The Montresor family motto was**

Ⓐ "Live and Let Live."

Ⓑ "No One Insults Me Without Punishment."

Ⓒ "No One Can Drink Too Much Wine."

Ⓓ "Do unto Others as You Would Have Them Do unto You."

## READING BETWEEN THE LINES

A *theme* is a "message" found in a literary work. An *inference* is a conclusion drawn from facts. Analyze the story by choosing the best answer to each question below.

**1. A theme for this story is**

Ⓐ people will do terrible things for a bottle of fine wine.

Ⓑ a cough can kill you.

Ⓒ having too much pride can get you into trouble.

Ⓓ revenge is the only way to make things even.

**2. What conclusion can you draw from paragraphs 16–25?**

Ⓐ Fortunato was too proud to allow Luchesi to see the Amontillado instead of him.

Ⓑ Luchesi knew more about wine than Fortunato.

Ⓒ Fortunato couldn't be bothered with helping Montresor, even though he loved Amontillado.

Ⓓ Montresor didn't want to waste Fortunato's time.

**3. What conclusion can you draw from paragraph 27?**

Ⓐ The servants were afraid of Montresor and always followed his orders.

Ⓑ Montresor was nervous about being alone in his house with Fortunato.

Ⓒ Montresor didn't want his servants to be home when he arrived with Fortunato.

Ⓓ The narrator was angry with his servants for disobeying his orders.

**4. It can be inferred from the story that**

Ⓐ Montresor was never punished for killing Fortunato.

Ⓑ Fortunato's family never noticed he was missing.

Ⓒ Montresor drank the Amontillado by himself.

Ⓓ Fortunato didn't learn his lesson about insulting others.

———■———

## DETERMINING CAUSE AND EFFECT

Choose the best answer for the following questions to show the relationship between *what* happened in the story (*effects*) and *why* those things happened (*causes*).

**1. Because Fortunato insulted him, Monstresor**

   Ⓐ refused to speak to him again.

   Ⓑ began to weep.

   Ⓒ forgave him.

   Ⓓ vowed revenge.

**2. What happened because Fortunato prided himself on being a wine expert?**

   Ⓐ Montresor used wine to lure him into his home.

   Ⓑ People often asked his advice on the type of wine to serve guests.

   Ⓒ He often insulted the wine his hosts tried to serve him.

   Ⓓ His friends often gave him fine wine as a gift.

**3. Why did Montresor choose walling Fortunato up in the vaults for his revenge?**

Pretend that you are interviewing Montresor. How would he answer this question? Write his reply on the lines below.

_____

_____

_____

_____

_____

**4. Why did Montresor stop his work and sit down upon the bones after completing the fourth row of bricks?**

   Ⓐ He was exhausted from the hard work.

   Ⓑ He wanted to listen to Fortunato's shaking of his chain with more enjoyment.

   Ⓒ He was having second thoughts about leaving Fortunato in the vault.

   Ⓓ The dampness of the catacombs was making it difficult for him to breathe.

*Nightmares and Cold Sweats*

## USING CONTEXT CLUES

Skilled readers can often find the meaning of unfamiliar words by using *context clues*. This means they study the way the words are used in the text. Use the context clues in the excerpts below to determine the meaning of the **bold-faced** words. Then choose the answer that best matches the meaning of the word.

**1.** "Sooner or later, I would be **avenged**."

*CLUE*: "Over the years, I had stood the thousand wrongs of Fortunato as I best could. But when he insulted me, I vowed revenge."

  Ⓐ repaid

  Ⓑ forgiven

  Ⓒ recognized

  Ⓓ punished

**2.** " 'And I was silly enough to pay the full Amontillado price without **consulting** you.' "

*CLUE*: " 'And I have my doubts about whether it truly is Amontillado or not. . . . You were not to be found, and I was fearful of losing a bargain.' "

  Ⓐ repaying

  Ⓑ doubting

  Ⓒ excusing

  Ⓓ asking

**3.** "The **feeble** light did not let us see its end."

*CLUE*: "Fortunato lifted up his dull torch. But it was in vain that he tried to see into the depths of the recess."

  Ⓐ weak

  Ⓑ bright

  Ⓒ expensive

  Ⓓ fine

**4.** "I began to **vigorously** wall up the entrance of the space."

*CLUE*: "As I said these words, I busied myself. . . . I made use of these materials and my trowel."

  Ⓐ timidly

  Ⓑ clumsily

  Ⓒ slowly

  Ⓓ energetically

# End-of-Unit Activities

**1. This unit is titled "The Dark Side of Human Nature."
Compare two people or groups of people from the stories
in this unit. Which do you think is more evil? Write the
characteristics of each person or group below. Then write
a paragraph justifying why you think one is more evil.**

**Person/Group 1** _____

Characteristics:

_____    _____

_____    _____

_____    _____


**Person/Group 2** _____

Characteristics:

_____    _____

_____    _____

_____    _____


I think _____ is more evil because _____

_____

_____

_____

_____

# End-of-Unit Activities

2. **Rank each of the stories in this unit, from the one you liked the most to the one you liked the least. Then write a paragraph describing why you liked the story you ranked *1* the best.**

**LESSON 5** Ranking _____

_____

_____

_____

_____

**LESSON 6** Ranking _____

_____

_____

_____

_____

**LESSON 7** Ranking _____

_____

_____

_____

_____

**LESSON 8** Ranking _____

_____

_____

_____

_____

Why did you like the story you ranked *1* the best?

_____

_____

_____

_____

# Words-Per-Minute Chart

## UNIT TWO

**Directions:**

Use the chart to find your words-per-minute reading speed. Refer to the reading time you recorded at the end of each story. Find your reading time in seconds along the left-hand side of the chart or minutes and seconds along the right-hand side of the chart. Your words-per-minute score will be listed next to the time in the column below the appropriate lesson number.

Seconds

Minutes and Seconds

| No. of Words | Lesson 5<br>2,354 | Lesson 6<br>1,803 | Lesson 7<br>1,835 | Lesson 8<br>2,357 | |
|---|---|---|---|---|---|
| 360 | 392 | 301 | 306 | 393 | 6:00 |
| 380 | 372 | 285 | 290 | 372 | 6:20 |
| 400 | 353 | 270 | 275 | 354 | 6:40 |
| 420 | 336 | 258 | 262 | 337 | 7:00 |
| 440 | 321 | 246 | 250 | 321 | 7:20 |
| 460 | 307 | 235 | 239 | 307 | 7:40 |
| 480 | 294 | 225 | 229 | 295 | 8:00 |
| 500 | 282 | 216 | 220 | 283 | 8:20 |
| 520 | 272 | 208 | 212 | 272 | 8:40 |
| 540 | 262 | 200 | 204 | 262 | 9:00 |
| 560 | 252 | 193 | 197 | 253 | 9:20 |
| 580 | 244 | 187 | 190 | 244 | 9:40 |
| 600 | 235 | 180 | 184 | 236 | 10:00 |
| 620 | 228 | 174 | 178 | 228 | 10:20 |
| 640 | 221 | 169 | 172 | 221 | 10:40 |
| 660 | 214 | 164 | 167 | 214 | 11:00 |
| 680 | 208 | 159 | 162 | 208 | 11:20 |
| 700 | 202 | 155 | 157 | 202 | 11:40 |
| 720 | 196 | 150 | 153 | 196 | 12:00 |
| 740 | 191 | 146 | 149 | 191 | 12:20 |
| 760 | 186 | 142 | 145 | 186 | 12:40 |
| 780 | 181 | 139 | 141 | 181 | 13:00 |
| 800 | 177 | 135 | 138 | 177 | 13:20 |
| 820 | 172 | 132 | 134 | 172 | 13:40 |
| 840 | 168 | 129 | 131 | 168 | 14:00 |
| 860 | 164 | 126 | 128 | 164 | 14:20 |
| 880 | 161 | 123 | 125 | 161 | 14:40 |
| 900 | 157 | 120 | 122 | 157 | 15:00 |
| 920 | 154 | 118 | 120 | 154 | 15:20 |
| 940 | 150 | 115 | 117 | 150 | 15:40 |
| 960 | 147 | 113 | 115 | 147 | 16:00 |
| 980 | 144 | 110 | 112 | 144 | 16:20 |
| 1,000 | 141 | 108 | 110 | 141 | 16:40 |
| 1,020 | 138 | 106 | 108 | 139 | 17:00 |
| 1,040 | 136 | 104 | 106 | 136 | 17:20 |
| 1,060 | 133 | 102 | 104 | 133 | 17:40 |
| 1,080 | 131 | 100 | 102 | 131 | 18:00 |
| 1,100 | 128 | 98 | 100 | 129 | 18:20 |
| 1,120 | 126 | 97 | 98 | 126 | 18:40 |
| 1,140 | 124 | 95 | 97 | 124 | 19:00 |
| 1,160 | 122 | 93 | 95 | 122 | 19:20 |
| 1,180 | 120 | 92 | 93 | 120 | 19:40 |
| 1,200 | 118 | 90 | 92 | 118 | 20:00 |
| 1,220 | 116 | 89 | 90 | 116 | 20:20 |
| 1,240 | 114 | 87 | 89 | 114 | 20:40 |
| 1,260 | 112 | 86 | 87 | 112 | 21:00 |
| 1,280 | 110 | 85 | 86 | 110 | 21:20 |
| 1,300 | 109 | 83 | 85 | 109 | 21:40 |
| 1,320 | 107 | 82 | 83 | 107 | 22:00 |
| 1,340 | 105 | 81 | 82 | 106 | 22:20 |
| 1,360 | 104 | 80 | 81 | 104 | 22:40 |
| 1,380 | 102 | 78 | 80 | 102 | 23:00 |
| 1,400 | 101 | 77 | 79 | 101 | 23:20 |
| 1,420 | 99 | 76 | 78 | 100 | 23:40 |
| 1,440 | 98 | 75 | 76 | 98 | 24:00 |

*Nightmares and Cold Sweats*

# UNIT THREE—

# a surplus
# of horror

# Dracula's Guest

Bram Stoker

As we prepared for our drive, the sun was shining brightly on Munich. The air was full of the joy of early summer. Herr Delbrück was the maître d'hôtel of the Quatre Saisons, where I was staying. Just as we were about to depart, he came down to the carriage. He wished me a pleasant drive, but he kept holding on to the handle of the carriage door.

[2]"Remember, you must be back by nightfall," he said to Johann, the coachman. "The sky looks bright. But there is a shiver in the north wind. That means there may be a sudden storm. But I am sure you will not be late." He smiled and added, "For you know what night it is."

[3]Johann answered with a forceful, "Yes, sir!"

[4]Touching his hat, Johann drove off quickly. When we had cleared the town, I signaled for him to stop.

[5]"Tell me, Johann," I said, "what is tonight?"

[6]He crossed himself and answered bluntly, "Walpurgisnacht."

[7]Then he took out his silver watch. It was an old-fashioned German watch as big as a turnip. He looked at it with a frown and gave a little impatient shrug of his shoulders. I realized that this was his way of politely complaining about the unnecessary delay.

[8]I sank back in the carriage and motioned for him to go on. He started off rapidly, as if to make up for lost time. I noticed that every now and then, the horses seemed to throw up their heads and sniff the air uneasily. Whenever that happened, I looked around in alarm.

[9]The road was bleak. We were crossing a rather high, windswept plateau. As we drove, I saw what appeared to be a little-used road that dipped through a small winding valley. It looked very pleasant there.

At the risk of offending Johann, I called him to a stop.

[10]When he had pulled up, I told him I would like to drive down that road. He made all sorts of excuses and kept crossing himself. This stirred my curiosity, so I asked him many questions. He answered as though fencing and repeatedly looked at his watch in protest.

[11]Finally, I said, "Well, Johann, I want to go down this road. I shall not ask you to come unless you like. But tell me why you do not want to go—that is all I ask."

[12]For his answer, he jumped from the box. He reached the ground so quickly that he must have thrown himself from his seat. Then he stretched out his hands appealingly and begged me not to go.

[13]There was just enough English mixed with his German for me to understand most of what he said. He always seemed just about to tell me something—the very idea of which seemed to frighten him. But each time he paused, crossed himself, and said, "Walpurgisnacht!"

[14]I tried to argue with him. But it was difficult to argue with a man when I did not know his language. He certainly had the better of me because of that. He began to speak in broken English. But he kept getting very excited and breaking into his native tongue. Every time he did so, he looked at his watch.

[15]The horses became restless and sniffed at the air again. At this, Johann grew very pale and looked around in a frightened way. Suddenly he jumped forward, took the horses by the bridles, and led them on some 20 feet.

[16]I followed and asked why he had done this. For an answer, he crossed himself. He pointed to the spot we had left. Then he drew the carriage in the direction of the other road, pointing to where the roads crossed.

[17]He said, first in German and then in English, "Buried him—him—what killed themselves."

[18]I remembered the old custom of burying people at crossroads who had committed suicide. "Ah, I see, a suicide. How interesting!" But, for the life of me, I could not make out why the horses were so frightened.

[19]While we were talking, we heard a sort of sound between a yelp and a bark. It sounded far off, but the horses got very nervous. It took Johann a long time to quiet them. He was pale, and he said, "It

sounds like a wolf. But yet there are no wolves here now."

[20]"No?" I said, questioning him. "Hasn't it been a long time since the wolves were so near the city?"

[21]"Long, long," he answered, "in the spring and summer. With this snow, the wolves couldn't have been here long."

[22]He petted the horses and tried to quiet them. Dark clouds drifted rapidly across the sky. The sunshine passed away. A breath of cold wind drifted past us. It was only a breath, however, and seemed more like a warning than a real wind. Then the sun came out brightly again. Johann looked under his lifted hand at the horizon.

[23]"The storm of snow, he comes before long time," he said. Then he looked at his watch again. He held the reins firmly, for the horses were still pawing the ground restlessly and shaking their heads. He climbed quickly to his seat as though the time had come for continuing our journey.

[24]I felt a little stubborn and did not get into the carriage at once.

[25]"Tell me," I said, "about this place where the road leads."

[26]He crossed himself again and mumbled a prayer before he answered, "It is unholy."

[27]"What is unholy?" I inquired.

[28]"The village."

[29]"Then there is a village?"

[30]"No, no. No one has lived there for hundreds of years."

[31]This stirred my curiosity. "But you said there was a village."

[32]"There was."

[33]"Where is it now?"

[34]At that, he burst into a long story in both German and English. The languages were so mixed up that I could not understand exactly what he said. But I understood that hundreds of years ago, people had died there. They had been buried in the ground. Later, sounds were heard under the clay. When the graves were opened, men and women were found rosy with life, their mouths red with blood.

[35]Of course, those who still lived there were in a hurry to save their own lives. So they fled to other places. They fled to where the living lived and the dead were dead and not—not—! (He seemed afraid to speak the last words.)

[36]As Johann went on with his story, he grew more and more excited. It seemed as if his imagination had taken hold. He

ended in a perfect fit of fear—white-faced, sweating, trembling, and looking around him fearfully. He seemed to expect that something dreadful would show itself there in the bright sunshine on the open plain. Finally, in complete despair and agony, he cried, "Walpurgisnacht!"

[37]He pointed to the carriage for me to get in. My English blood rose at this. Standing back, I said, "You are afraid, Johann—you are afraid. Go home. I shall return alone. The walk will do me good."

[38]The carriage door was open. I took from the seat my oak walking stick, which I always carry on my travels. I closed the door. Pointing back to Munich, I said, "Go home, Johann. Walpurgisnacht doesn't worry Englishmen."

[39]The horses were now more restless than ever, and Johann was trying to hold them in. Excitedly, he begged me not to do anything so foolish. I pitied the poor fellow. He was deeply serious, but I could not help laughing.

[40]His English was quite gone now. In his anxiety, Johann had forgotten that his only means of making me understand was to speak my language. He jabbered away in his native German. It became a little tedious. After ordering Johann to go home, I turned to take the crossroad into the valley.

[41]With a hopeless gesture, Johann turned his horses toward Munich. I leaned on my stick and looked after him. He went slowly along the road for a while. Then a tall, thin man came over the hill. I could see that much in the distance.

[42]When the man drew near the horses, they began to jump and kick about. They screamed with terror. Johann could not hold them in. They bolted down the road, running away madly. I watched them go out of sight and looked again for the stranger. But I found that he, too, was gone.

[43]With a light heart, I turned down the side road. It went into the deepening valley that Johann had feared. As far as I could tell, there was not the slightest reason for him to feel so. I suppose I tramped for a couple of hours without thinking of time or distance. Certainly, I did not see a person or a house.

[44]So far as the place was concerned, it was desolation itself. But I did not much notice this until I turned a bend in the road and came upon an area that was scattered with trees. It was then that I recognized my mood had been much changed

by the desolation of the region.

[45]I sat down to rest myself and began to look around. It struck me that it was much colder than it had been at the beginning of my walk. There seemed to be a sort of sighing sound around me. Now and then, from high overhead, came a sort of muffled roar.

[46]I noticed thick clouds drifting rapidly across the sky. There were signs of a coming storm in some high layer of the air. I was a little chilly. Thinking it was from sitting still, I started my journey again.

[47]The land I traveled on now was much more picturesque. There were no striking objects that the eye might single out. But in all there was a charm of beauty.

[48]I took little notice of time until the deepening twilight forced itself upon me. Then I began to think of how I would find my way home now that the brightness of the day had gone. The air was cold, and the drifting clouds high overhead were more visible. They were joined by a faraway rushing sound. And I seemed to hear, at times, the mysterious cry that the driver had said came from a wolf.

[49]I waited for a while. I had said I would see the deserted village, so I went on. I soon came upon a wide stretch of open country that was enclosed in hills all around. The hillsides were covered with trees that spread down to the plain. The trees dotted the gentler slopes that appeared here and there. I followed the winding of the road with my eye. I saw that it curved close to one of the thickest clumps of trees and was lost behind it.

[50]As I looked, there came a cold shiver in the air, and the snow began to fall. I thought of the miles and miles of bleak country I had passed. Then I hurried to seek the shelter of the wood before me. The sky grew darker and darker. The snow fell faster and heavier. The earth before and around me became a glistening white carpet. And the further edge was lost in misty vagueness.

[51]The road was here, but it was rough. In a little while, I found that I must have strayed from it. For I suddenly missed having the hard surface underfoot, and my feet sank deeper in the grass and moss.

[52]Then the wind grew stronger and blew with increasing force. I was happy to run before it. The air became icy cold, and despite my exertion, I began to suffer.

[53]The snow was falling thickly. It whirled around me in such rapid

*Nightmares and Cold Sweats*

swirls that I could hardly keep my eyes open. The heavens were torn to pieces by bursts of lightning. In the flashes, I could see a great mass of trees ahead of me, chiefly yew and cypress. They were all heavily covered with snow.

[54]Soon I was in the shelter of the trees. In the comparative silence, I could hear the rush of the wind overhead, and the blackness of the storm blended into the darkness of the night. The storm seemed to be passing away. It now came in isolated fierce puffs or blasts. At such moments, the weird sound of the wolf was echoed by many similar sounds around me.

[55]Now and again, a straggling ray of moonlight came through the black mass of drifting cloud. It lit up the area. I saw that I was at the edge of the thick mass of trees. And, as the snow ceased to fall, I walked out from the shelter. I began to look around more closely.

[56]I had passed many old foundations. It seemed to me that among them a house might still be standing. But I figured I could find some sort of shelter, even in ruins, for a while. As I skirted around the wooded area, I found that a low wall encircled it. Following this, I presently found an opening.

[57]Here the cypresses formed an alley leading up to a square mass. It was some kind of building. Just as I caught sight of this, however, the drifting clouds hid the moon. I passed up the path in darkness. The wind must have grown colder. I shivered as I walked. But there was hope of shelter, so I soldiered on.

[58]I stopped, for there was a sudden stillness. The storm had passed. Perhaps echoing nature's silence, my heart ceased to beat for a moment. Suddenly, the moonlight broke through the clouds and showed me that I was in a graveyard. The square object before me was a massive tomb of marble. The tomb was as white as the snow that lay on and all around it.

[59]With the moonlight came a fierce sigh of the storm. The blizzard resumed its course with a long, low howl. It sounded like many dogs or wolves. I was awed and shocked.

[60]I felt the cold steadily grow upon me until it gripped me by the heart. The flood of moonlight still fell on the marble tomb, but the storm gave further signs of renewing.

[61]Driven by some sort of fascination, I approached the tomb to see what it was. I wondered why such a thing stood alone in such a

place. I walked around it and read in German:

COUNTESS DOLINGEN OF GRATZ

IN STYRIA

SOUGHT AND FOUND DEATH

1801

[62]The structure was made up of a few vast blocks of stone. On top of the tomb was a great iron spike or stake. It seemed to be driven through solid marble. Carved in great Russian letters was this saying: "The dead travel fast."

[63]There was something uncanny about the whole thing. It gave me a turn and made me feel quite faint. I began to wish, for the first time, that I had taken Johann's advice. Then a thought struck me in a most mysterious way and with a terrible shock. This was Walpurgis Night!

[64]Walpurgis Night was when, according to the beliefs of millions of people, the devil was afoot. It was when the graves opened and the dead came forth and walked. It was when all evil things of earth and air and water celebrated.

[65]This was the very place the driver had specifically stayed away from. This was the deserted village of centuries ago. This was where the suicides lay. And this was the place where I was alone and weak.

[66]I was shivering in a cloud of snow with another wild storm gathering over me! I needed all of my beliefs—all the religion I had been taught. It took all of my courage not to give way to an attack of fright.

[67]And now, a perfect tornado burst upon me. The ground shook as though thousands of horses thundered across it. This time, the storm brought hailstones that beat down leaf and branch. They made the shelter of cypresses of no more use than if their stems were standing corn.

[68]I rushed to the nearest tree, but I was soon glad to leave it. I sought the only spot that seemed to offer shelter, the deep doorway of the marble tomb. I crouched against the massive bronze door, where I gained a certain amount of protection from the onslaught of hailstones. Now they only drove against me whenever they bounced off the ground or the side of the marble.

[69]As I leaned against the door, it moved slightly and opened inward. The shelter of even a tomb was welcome in that cruel tempest. I was about to enter when a flash of forked lightning lit up the whole of the heavens.

[70]My eyes were turned toward the darkness of the tomb. In that instant, as I am a living man, I saw a beautiful woman. She had rounded cheeks and red lips. And she was seemingly sleeping on a bier.

[71]As the thunder broke overhead, I was grasped as if by the hand of a giant and hurled out into the storm. The whole thing was sudden. Before I could feel the shock, moral as well as physical, I felt the hailstones beating me down. At the same time, I had a powerful feeling that I was not alone.

[72]I looked toward the tomb. Just then came another blinding flash. It seemed to strike the iron stake on top of the tomb and pour through to the earth. The blast crumbled the marble with a burst of flame. The dead woman rose for a moment of agony while she was caught in the flame. Her bitter scream of pain was drowned in the thunder crash.

[73]The last thing I heard was this mingling of dreadful sound. Again I was seized by the giant grasp and dragged away. Brutal hailstones hit me, and the air echoed with the howling of wolves.

[74]The last sight that I remembered was a vague, white, moving mass. It was as if all the graves around me had sent out the phantoms of their sheeted dead. They were closing in on me through the white cloudiness of the driving hail.

[75]Eventually, I came back to my senses. Then I felt a dreadful sense of weariness. For a time I remembered nothing, but my awareness slowly returned. My feet were in terrible pain, yet I could not move them. They seemed to be numb.

[76]There was an icy feeling at the back of my neck and all down my spine. My ears, like my feet, were dead—yet they were in pain. But there was a sense of warmth in my breast that was, by comparison, delicious. It was a nightmare—a physical nightmare, if one may use such an expression. For some heavy weight on my chest made it difficult for me to breathe.

[77]This period of tiredness seemed to last a long time. As it faded away, I must have slept or fainted. Then came a sort of disgust, like the first stage of seasickness. I had a wild desire to be free from something—I knew not what. A vast stillness surrounded me, as though the whole world was asleep or dead. The silence was only broken by a low panting that sounded as though some animal was close to me.

*The vast stillness was only broken by a low panting that sounded as though some animal was close.*

[78]I felt a warm rasping at my throat. Then I became aware of the awful truth. It chilled me to my heart and sent the blood surging up through my brain. Some great animal was lying on me and licking my throat. I feared to stir, for some instinct told me to lie still.

[79]But the brute seemed to realize that there was some change in me. It raised its head. I saw above me the two flaming eyes of a gigantic wolf. Sharp, white teeth gleamed in its red, gaping mouth. I could feel its hot breath upon me.

[80]I remembered no more for another spell of time. Then I became aware of a low growl, followed by a yelp. This pattern was repeated again and again.

[81]Then I heard a faraway "Hello! Hello!" that sounded like many voices calling in unison. I raised my head cautiously. I looked in the direction from which the sound came, but the cemetery blocked my view. The wolf continued its strange yelping.

[82]A red glare began to move around the grove of cypresses, as though following the sound. As the voices drew closer, the wolf yelped faster and louder. I was afraid to make either sound or motion.

[83]The red glow came nearer. It shone over the white gloom that stretched into the darkness around me. Then all at once from beyond the trees appeared a troop of horsemen. They came at a trot, and they were bearing torches. I could tell that they were soldiers by their caps and long military cloaks.

*Nightmares and Cold Sweats*

[84]The wolf rose from my breast and headed toward the cemetery. I saw one of the horsemen raise his rifle and take aim. Another horseman aimed, and I heard the ball whiz over my head. He had evidently mistaken me for the wolf.

[85]Another soldier sighted and shot the animal as it tried to slink away. Then the troop rode forward at a gallop. Some came toward me. Others followed the wolf as it disappeared among the snow-clad cypresses.

[86]I tried to move as they drew nearer. Although I could see and hear all that went on around me, I was powerless. Two or three of the soldiers jumped from their horses and knelt beside me. One of them raised my head and placed his hand over my heart.

[87]"Good news, men!" he cried. "His heart still beats!"

[88]Someone poured a little brandy down my throat. It put some life back into me. I was able to fully open my eyes and look around. Lights and shadows were moving among the trees, and I heard men call to one another. They drew together, whispering in frightened voices. The lights flashed as the others came pouring out of the cemetery. They rode recklessly, like men gone mad.

[89]The farther riders came close to us. Those who were already nearby asked them eagerly, "Well, have you found him?"

[90]The reply rang out hurriedly, "No! No! Come away quick—quick! This is no place to stay, and on this of all nights!"

[91]"What was it?" The question was asked in many tones of voice. Many different and unclear answers came. It seemed as though the men were moved by some common wish to speak. Yet they were held back from saying their thoughts by some common fear.

[92]"It—it—indeed!" jabbered one. His wits had plainly given out for the moment.

[93]"A wolf—and yet not a wolf!" shouted another.

[94]"No use trying for him without the sacred bullet," a third remarked in a more ordinary manner.

[95]"It serves us right for coming out on this night! We have truly earned our thousand marks!" were the outcries of a fourth.

[96]"There was blood on the broken marble," said another after a pause. "The lightning never brought that there. And for him—is he safe?

Look at his throat! See, men, the wolf has been lying on him and keeping his blood warm."

[97]The officer looked at my throat and replied, "He is all right. The skin is not pierced. What does it all mean? If the wolf had not been yelping, we would never have found this fellow."

[98]"What became of it?" asked the man who was holding up my head. He seemed the least panic-stricken of the party. His hands were steady. On his sleeve was the chevron of a low-ranking officer.

[99]"It went to its home," answered the other, whose long face was pale. He actually shook with terror as he glanced around him. "There are enough graves there in which it may lie. Come, men—come quickly! Let us leave this cursed spot."

[100]The officer raised me to a sitting position as he uttered a word of command. Then several men placed me upon a horse. He sprang to the saddle behind me and took me in his arms. He gave the word to go forward. Turning our faces away from the cypresses, we rode away in swift, military order.

[101]As yet my tongue refused its job, and I was helplessly silent. I must have fallen asleep. The next thing I remembered was finding myself standing up. I was supported by a soldier on each side of me. It was almost broad daylight.

[102]To the north, a red streak of sunlight was reflected in the waste of snow. It made a path like blood. The officer was telling the men to say nothing of what they had seen. He told them to say that they had found an English stranger, guarded by a large dog.

[103]"Dog! That was no dog," cut in the man who had shown such fear. "I think I know a wolf when I see one."

[104]The young officer answered calmly, "I said a dog."

[105]"Dog!" repeated the other ironically. It was evident that his courage was rising with the sun. Pointing to me, he said, "Look at his throat. Is that the work of a dog, master?"

[106]Instinctively, I raised my hand to my throat. As I touched it, I cried out in pain. The men crowded around to look, some stooping from their saddles.

[107]And again came the calm voice of the young officer. "A dog, as I said. If anything else were said, we would only be laughed at."

[108]I was then mounted behind a

trooper, and we rode on into the suburbs of Munich. We came across a stray carriage into which I was lifted. It was driven off to the Quatre Saisons. The young officer rode along with me, and a trooper followed with his horse. The others rode off to their barracks.

[109]When we arrived, Herr Delbrück rushed quickly down the steps to meet me. It was apparent that he had been watching from within. Taking me by both hands, he carefully led me in. The officer saluted me and was turning to withdraw. When I saw that he was about to leave, I insisted that he come to my rooms.

[110]Over a glass of wine, I warmly thanked him and his brave horsemen for saving me. He replied simply that he was more than glad. He said that Herr Delbrück had already taken steps to please everyone in the searching party. At that vague statement, the maître d'hôtel smiled. Then the officer said that he had work to do and left.

[111]"But, Herr Delbrück," I inquired "how and why was it that the soldiers searched for me?"

[112]He shrugged his shoulders as if to belittle his own deed. He replied, "I was lucky. I got permission to ask for volunteers from the commander of the regiment in which I served."

[113]"But how did you know I was lost?" I asked.

[114]"The driver came here with the remains of his carriage. It had been upset when the horses ran away."

[115]"But surely you would not send a search party of soldiers merely because of that?"

[116]"Oh, no!" he answered. "But before the coachman arrived, I had this telegram from the count whose guest you are." And he took from his pocket a telegram. He handed it to me, and I read:

BISTRITZ, TRANYSLVANIA

BE CAREFUL OF MY GUEST— HIS SAFETY IS MOST PRECIOUS TO ME. SHOULD ANYTHING HAPPEN TO HIM, OR IF HE BE MISSED, SPARE NOTHING TO FIND HIM. PROTECT HIS SAFETY. HE IS ENGLISH AND THEREFORE ADVENTUROUS. THERE ARE OFTEN DANGERS FROM SNOW AND WOLVES AT NIGHT. LOSE NOT A MOMENT IF YOU SUSPECT HARM TO HIM. I ANSWER YOUR CARE WITH MY WEALTH.

DRACULA

[117]As I held the telegram in my hand, the room whirled around me. If the watchful maître d'hôtel had not caught me, I would have fallen.

There was something so strange in all this, something strange and impossible to imagine. There grew in me a sense of my being in some way the sport of two opposing forces.

[118]The mere idea seemed to paralyze me. I was certainly under some form of mysterious protection. From a distant country, a message had come. It was a message that took me out of the danger of sleep and the jaws of the wolf. And it had come in the very nick of time.

---

*If you have been timing your reading speed for this story, record your time below.*

_____ : _____

**Minutes        Seconds**

---

*Nightmares and Cold Sweats*

## UNDERSTANDING THE MAIN IDEA

The following questions will demonstrate your understanding of what the story is about, or the *main idea*. Choose the best answer for each question.

**1. This story is mainly about**

&#9398; a man whose curiosity got him into trouble.

&#9399; old German superstitions.

&#9400; a wolf that saved a man's life.

&#9401; what a good host Count Dracula was.

**2. This story could have been titled**

&#9398; "A Snowy Adventure."

&#9399; "Fun in the Graveyard."

&#9400; "Alone on Walpurgis Night."

&#9401; "The Life of Count Dracula."

**3. Which detail best supports the main idea of the story?**

&#9398; A winter storm was on its way.

&#9399; Herr Delbrück told the coachman to be back by nightfall.

&#9400; The horses seemed to throw up their heads and sniff the air uneasily.

&#9401; The Englishman sent the coachman away and set off for the old village alone.

**4. Find another detail that supports the main idea of this story. Write it on the lines below.**

_____

_____

_____

## RECALLING FACTS

The following questions will test how well you remember the facts in the story you just read. Choose the best answer for each question.

**1. According to Johann, the abandoned road led to**

&#9398; an old village where the dead had come back to life.

&#9399; Count Dracula's castle in the woods.

&#9400; an old village wiped out by poverty.

&#9401; a large wolves' den.

**2. Inside the tomb, the Englishman thought he saw**

&#9398; Count Dracula himself.

&#9399; a wolf snarling at him.

&#9400; a man rising from the grave.

&#9401; a beautiful woman sleeping.

**3. The party of soldiers agreed**

&#9398; that their minds had been playing tricks on them.

&#9399; to leave the Englishman in the graveyard.

&#9400; to tell their story to the newspaper.

&#9401; not to tell anyone about the wolf.

**4. Herr Delbrück received a mysterious telegram telling him to**

&#9398; fire the coachman.

&#9399; protect the Englishman's safety.

&#9400; take shelter from the winter storm.

&#9401; visit the graveyard at midnight.

## READING BETWEEN THE LINES

A *theme* is a "message" found in a literary work. An *inference* is a conclusion drawn from facts. Analyze the story by choosing the best answer to each question below.

**1. A theme for this story is**

Ⓐ it wise to believe in superstitions.

Ⓑ always listen to what the coachman says.

Ⓒ too much curiosity can get a person into trouble.

Ⓓ wolves are dangerous creatures.

**2. What conclusion can you draw from paragraphs 37–40?**

Ⓐ The Englishman was lazy and didn't like to exercise.

Ⓑ Johann wasn't worried about the Englishman's safety.

Ⓒ The Englishman was very superstitious.

Ⓓ Johann's worries didn't concern the Englishman.

**3. What conclusion can you draw from paragraphs 64–66?**

Ⓐ The Englishman's religion celebrated Walpurgis Night as a major religious holiday.

Ⓑ The Englishman's religious beliefs taught him not to believe in Walpurgis Night.

Ⓒ Now that he was alone in the graveyard at night, the Englishman wasn't afraid.

Ⓓ The coachman's story about Walpurgis Night had come true.

**4. It can be inferred from the story that**

Ⓐ Count Dracula saved the Englishman's life.

Ⓑ Count Dracula wanted to meet with the Englishman so he could suck his blood.

Ⓒ Count Dracula did not really exist.

Ⓓ Count Dracula wanted the Englishman to get lost in the snow.

## DETERMINING CAUSE AND EFFECT

Choose the best answer for the following questions to show the relationship between *what* happened in the story (*effects*) and *why* those things happened (*causes*).

**1. Because Johann told him the story about the abandoned village,**

Ⓐ the Englishman became very curious to see where it had once stood.

Ⓑ the horses became more and more anxious.

Ⓒ Count Dracula came looking for the Englishman to give him a tour.

Ⓓ the wolves circled the carriage.

**2. What happened because the Englishman kept looking for the village in spite of the storm and falling darkness?**

Ⓐ He got lost in a snowstorm and froze to death.

Ⓑ Count Dracula had to show him the way back to Munich.

Ⓒ He lost his way in the woods and wound up in a graveyard.

Ⓓ The coachman had to chase after him with the carriage.

**3. Why did the soldiers agree to say they'd seen a dog, rather than a wolf?**

Ⓐ None of them wanted to believe that what they'd seen had really happened.

Ⓑ They were afraid Count Dracula would come after them if they told the truth.

Ⓒ They knew that if anything else were said, they would be laughed at.

Ⓓ They knew wolves weren't likely to be found in that part of the country.

**4. Why did the wolf run away?**

Ⓐ It was tired of drinking the Englishman's blood.

Ⓑ Count Dracula chased it away.

Ⓒ It was almost sunrise.

Ⓓ The soldiers shot at it.

## USING CONTEXT CLUES

Skilled readers can often find the meaning of unfamiliar words by using *context clues*. This means they study the way the words are used in the text. Use the context clues in the excerpts below to determine the meaning of the **bold-faced** words. Then choose the answer that best matches the meaning of the word.

**1.** "Just as we were about to **depart**, [Herr Delbrück] came down to the carriage."

*CLUE*: "As we prepared for our drive, the sun was shining brightly on Munich."

   Ⓐ leave

   Ⓑ run

   Ⓒ decide

   Ⓓ arrive

**2.** "Finally, in complete **despair** and agony, [Johann] cried, 'Walpurgisnacht!' "

*CLUE*: "As Johann went on with his story, he grew more and more excited. . . . He ended in a perfect fit of fear—white-faced, sweating, trembling, and looking around him fearfully. He seemed to expect that something dreadful would show itself there . . ."

   Ⓐ gratitude

   Ⓑ triumph

   Ⓒ distress

   Ⓓ impatience

**3.** "The land I traveled on now was much more **picturesque**."

*CLUE*: "There were no striking objects that the eye might single out. But in all there was a charm of beauty."

   Ⓐ private

   Ⓑ well-traveled

   Ⓒ dull

   Ⓓ beautiful

**4.** "The shelter of even a tomb was welcome in that cruel **tempest**." (paragraph 69)

Write what you think the **bold-faced** word means. Then, record the context clues that led you to this definition.

Meaning:

_____

_____

_____

Context Clues:

_____

_____

_____

—■—

# The Monkey's Paw

### W.W. Jacobs

The night outside was cold and wet. But inside the small parlor of Laburman Villa, the blinds were drawn and the fire burned brightly.

[2] Father and son played a game of chess. The father had ideas that the game demanded daring moves. So he often placed his king in dangerous positions on the board. His moves even led the white-haired lady knitting peacefully by the fire to comment.

[3] "Listen to that wind," said Mr. White. He had just seen a fatal mistake he had made. It was too late to take the move back. But, by speaking, he tried to prevent his son, Herbert, from seeing the error.

[4] "I'm listening," said Herbert. He grimly studied the board as he stretched out his hand. "Check."

[5] "I should hardly think that he'd come tonight," said Mr. White. He spoke with his hand poised over the board.

[6] "Mate," replied Herbert.

[7] "That's the worst of living so far out," cried Mr. White. His tone was suddenly unexpectedly violent.

[8] "Of all the beastly, slushy, out-of-the-way places to live, this is the worst. The pathway's a swamp and the road's flooded.

[9] "I don't know what people are thinking about. I suppose because only two houses on the road are rented, they think it doesn't matter."

[10] "Never mind, dear," said Mrs. White soothingly. "Perhaps you'll win the next one."

[11] Mr. White looked up sharply. He was just in time to catch a knowing glance pass between mother and son. The words died away on his lips. He hid a guilty grin in his thin gray beard.

[12] "There he is," said Herbert. The gate banged loudly and heavy footsteps came toward the door.

[13] The old man rose in polite haste. He opened the door and was heard sympathizing with the new arrival. The new arrival also sympathized with himself.

[14] Mrs. White overheard and said, "Tut, tut!" She coughed gently as her husband entered the room. A tall, sturdy man with beady eyes and a red face followed him.

[15] "Sergeant-Major Morris," Mr. White said, introducing the man.

[16] The sergeant-major shook hands. Then he took a seat by the fire. He watched contentedly while his host got out whiskey and glasses and put a small copper kettle on the fire.

[17] After the third glass, the sergeant-major's eyes got brighter. He began to talk. The little family circle listened eagerly to this visitor from distant lands. He squared his broad shoulders in the chair. Then he spoke of strange scenes and brave deeds. He also told of wars and plagues and strange peoples.

[18] "It's been 21 years," said Mr. White. He nodded at his wife and son. "When Morris went away, he was just a young boy in the warehouse. Now look at him."

[19] "He doesn't look as though his travels have harmed him," Mrs. White said politely.

[20] "I'd like to go to India myself," said the old man. "Just to look around a bit, you know."

[21] "It's better where you are," said Morris, shaking his head. He put the empty glass down. Sighing softly, he shook his head again.

[22] "I should like to see those old temples and fakirs and jugglers," said the old man. "What was that you started telling me the other day? Was it about a monkey's paw or something, Morris?"

[23] "Nothing," said Morris hastily. "Anyway, it's nothing worth hearing."

[24] "Monkey's paw?" said Mrs. White curiously.

[25] "Well, it's just a bit of what you might call magic, perhaps," said Morris casually.

[26] His three listeners leaned forward eagerly. The visitor absentmindedly put his empty glass to his lips. Then he set it down again. His host filled it for him.

[27] Morris fumbled in his pocket. He explained, "To look at it, it's just

an ordinary little paw, dried like a mummy."

[28]He took something out of his pocket and held it out. Mrs. White drew back with a disgusted look. But her son took it and examined it curiously.

[29]"And what is there special about it?" asked Mr. White. He

*A fakir put a spell on the paw.*

took the paw from his son. After examining it, he placed it on the table.

[30]"It had a spell put on it by an old fakir," said Morris. "He was a very holy man. He wanted to show that fate ruled people's lives. And he wanted to prove that those who interfered with fate did so to their own sorrow.

[31]"So the fakir put a spell on the paw. He gave it the power to grant three separate men three wishes each."

[32]Their visitor's manner was so impressive that the family realized that their laughter jarred somewhat.

[33]"Well, why don't you make three wishes, sir?" said Herbert White cleverly.

[34]The soldier stared at him the way that adults usually looked at presumptuous youths. "I have," he said quietly. His blotchy face turned white.

[35]"And did you really have the three wishes granted?" asked Mrs. White.

[36]"I did," said Morris. His glass tapped against his strong teeth.

[37]"And has anybody else wished?" asked Mrs. White.

[38]"The first man had his three wishes, yes," was the reply. "I don't

know what the first two were. But the third was for death. That's how I got the paw."

[39] His tones were so grave that a hush fell upon the group.

[40] "If you've had your three wishes, then it's no good to you now, Morris," said the old man at last. "What do you keep it for?"

[41] The soldier shook his head. "A silly impulse, I suppose," he said slowly. "I did have some idea of selling it. But I don't think I will. It has caused enough mischief already.

[42] "Besides, people won't buy it. They think it's a fairy tale, some of them. And those who do think anything of it want to try it first and pay me later."

[43] "What if you could have another three wishes?" said the old man. He eyed Morris closely. "Would you have them?"

[44] "I don't know," said the soldier. "I don't know."

[45] He took the paw and dangled it between his finger and thumb. Then suddenly he threw it onto the fire. White, with a slight cry, bent down and snatched it off.

[46] "Better let it burn," said the soldier solemnly.

[47] "If you don't want it, Morris," said the old man, "give it to me."

[48] "I won't," said his friend stubbornly. "I threw it on the fire. If you keep it, don't blame me for what happens. Toss it on the fire again, like a sensible man."

[49] White shook his head and examined his new possession closely. "How do you do it?" he asked.

[50] "Hold it up in your right hand and wish aloud," said the sergeant-major. "But I warn you of the consequences."

[51] "Sounds like Arabian Nights," said Mrs. White. She rose and began to set the table for supper. "Don't you think you might wish for four pairs of hands for me?" she teased.

[52] Her husband drew the talisman from his pocket. Then the family burst into laughter as Morris, with a look of alarm on his face, caught Mr. White by the arm.

[53] "If you must wish," he said gruffly, "wish for something sensible."

[54] Mr. White dropped it back into his pocket. Then, placing chairs, he motioned his friend to the table.

[55] During the business of supper, the talisman was partly forgotten.

*Nightmares and Cold Sweats*

Afterward, the three sat listening spellbound to more of the soldier's adventures in India.

[56]Much later their guest left to catch the last train. As the door closed behind Morris, Herbert said, "If the tale about the paw is as truthful as the others he told us, we won't make much from it."

[57]"Did you give him anything for it, Father?" asked Mrs. White. She watched her husband closely.

[58]"A little something," said Mr. White, blushing slightly. "He didn't want it, but I made him take it. And he urged me again to throw the paw away."

[59]"Of course," said Herbert, with pretended horror. "Why, we're going to be rich and famous and happy. Wish to be an emperor to begin with, Father. Then you won't be henpecked."

[60]Herbert darted round the table chased by his mother. The maligned Mrs. White pursued him with a chair slipcover.

[61]Mr. White took the paw from his pocket and eyed it doubtfully. "I don't know what to wish for, and that's a fact," he said slowly. "It seems to me I've got all I want."

[62]Herbert put his arm on his father's shoulder. "If you only could pay off the house. You'd be quite happy then, wouldn't you?" he said. "Well, wish for 200 pounds then. That'll just do it."

[63]Mr. White held up the talisman. He smiled, embarrassed at his own credulity. Herbert sat at the piano and struck a few impressive chords. His solemn face was somewhat spoiled by a wink at his mother.

[64]"I wish for 200 pounds," said the old man distinctly.

[65]A fine crash from the piano met the words. The chord was interrupted by a trembling cry from the old man. His wife and son ran toward him.

[66]"It moved," he cried. He gazed in disgust at the paw as it lay on the floor. "When I wished, it twisted in my hands like a snake."

[67]"Well, I don't see the money," said Herbert. He picked up the paw and placed it on the table. "And I bet I never will."

[68]"It must have been your imagination, Father," said Mrs. White. She looked at him anxiously.

[69]He shook his head. "Never mind, though. There's no harm done. But it gave me a shock all the same."

[70]They sat down by the fire again while father and son finished their pipes. Outside the wind was blowing

harder than ever. Mr. White jumped nervously when a door banged upstairs.

[71]An unusual and depressing silence settled upon all three. It lasted until the old couple rose to retire for the night.

[72]"I expect you'll find the cash tied up in a bag in the middle of your bed," said Herbert as he said good night. "And there'll be something horrible squatting on top of the closet watching as you pocket your foul gains."

[73]He sat alone in the darkness. Gazing at the dying fire, he saw faces in it. The last face was so horrible and apelike that he gazed at it in amazement.

[74]It got so real that, with a little uneasy laugh, he felt on the table for a glass of water to throw at it. His hand grasped the monkey's paw instead. With a little shiver, he wiped his hand on his coat and went to bed.

[75]Next morning, this winter sun streamed over the breakfast table. In that bright light, Herbert laughed at his fears. The mood of last night was gone. Now there was an air of everyday wholesomeness about the room.

[76]The dirty, shriveled little paw had been carelessly tossed on a cabinet. It lay there as if its virtues were hardly to be believed.

[77]"I suppose all old soldiers are the same," said Mrs. White. "The idea of our listening to such nonsense! How could wishes be granted in this day and age? And if they could, how could 200 pounds hurt you, Father?"

[78]"Might drop on his head from the sky," said the frivolous Herbert.

[79]"Morris said that the things happen naturally," said his father. "You might just think it's a coincidence."

[80]"Well, don't break into the money before I come back," said Herbert as he rose from the table. "I'm afraid it'll turn you into a mean, greedy man. We'd have to kick you out of the family."

[81]His mother laughed. Following Herbert to the door, she watched him walk down the road. Returning to the breakfast table, she thought merrily about her husband's credulity.

[82]All of this did not stop her from scurrying to the door when the postman knocked. Nor did it stop her from muttering about drunken sergeant-majors when she found that the mail was just a tailor's bill.

[83]She brought the topic up again when they sat down to dinner. "I expect Herbert will have some more of his funny remarks when he comes home," she said.

[84]"That's very likely," said Mr. White, pouring himself out some beer. "But even so, the thing moved in my hand. I'll swear to that."

[85]"You thought it did," said the old lady soothingly.

[86]"I say it did," replied the old man. "There was no thought about it. I had just—what's the matter?"

[87]His wife made no reply. She was watching the mysterious movements of a man outside. This stranger was peering in an undecided way at the house. He appeared to be trying to make up his mind to enter.

[88]Mrs. White was still thinking about the 200 pounds. So naturally she noticed that the stranger was well dressed. She also noted his silk hat was shiny and new.

[89]Three times the man paused at the gate. Then he began to walk by.

[90]The fourth time he stood with his hand upon the gate. Then, with sudden resolution, he flung the gate open and walked up the path.

[91]At the same moment, Mrs. White placed her hands behind her. She hurriedly untied her apron and put it beneath a chair cushion.

[92]She brought the stranger into the room. He seemed ill at ease. He gazed at Mrs. While out of the corner of his eye. And he listened in a preoccupied way as she apologized for the room's appearance and her husband's coat. She explained that he usually only wore it in the garden.

[93]Mrs. White then waited patiently for the stranger to bring up his business. But he was, at first, strangely silent.

[94]"I—was asked to call," he said at last. He stooped down and picked a piece of cotton from his trousers. "I come from Maw and Meggins."

[95]The old lady jumped. "Is anything the matter?" she asked breathlessly. "Has anything happened to Herbert? What is it? What is it?"

[96]Her husband stepped in. "There, there, Mother," he said hastily. "Sit down, and don't jump to conclusions. You've not brought bad news, I'm sure, sir." He eyed the stranger hopefully.

[97]"I'm sorry—" began the visitor.

[98]"Is he hurt?" demanded the mother.

[99]The visitor bowed in agreement. "Badly hurt," he said quietly. "But he's not in any pain."

[100]"Oh, thank God!" said the old woman, clasping her hands. "Thank God for that. Thank—"

[101]She stopped suddenly as the sinister meaning of the man's words dawned upon her. She saw the awful confirmation of her fears when the man turned his face away.

[102]Catching her breath, she turned to her slower-witted husband. She laid her trembling old hand upon his. There was a long silence.

[103]"He was caught in the machinery," said the visitor at last, in a low voice.

[104]"Caught in the machinery," repeated Mr. White in a dazed manner. "Yes."

[105]He sat staring blankly out the window. He took his wife's hand between his own. He pressed it as he used to do when they were courting nearly forty years ago.

[106]"He was the only one left to us," he said, turning gently to the visitor. "It is hard."

[107]The other coughed. Rising, he walked slowly to the window. "The firm wished me to express their sincere sympathy with you in your great loss," he said. He spoke without looking around.

[108]"I beg that you will understand I am only their employee. I am merely obeying orders."

[109]There was no reply. The old woman's face was white, her eyes staring. Her breath could not be heard. On the husband's face was a look such as the sergeant might have carried into his first battle.

[110]"I am to say that Maw and Meggins refuse to take any responsibility," continued the stranger. "They admit no liability at all.

[111]"But, out of regard for your son's services, they want to make a gesture. They wish to present you with a certain sum as compensation."

[112]Mr. White dropped his wife's hand. Rising to his feet, he gazed in horror at his visitor. His dry lips shaped the words, "How much?"

[113]"Two hundred pounds," was the answer.

[114]Unconscious of his wife's shriek, the old man smiled faintly. He reached out his hands and dropped in a heap on the floor.

[115]The huge new cemetery lay some two miles away. There the Whites buried their dead son. Then

they came back to a house full of shadow and silence.

[116]It was all over so quickly that at first they could hardly realize it. They continued to wait, as though expecting something else to happen. They waited for something that would lighten this load, too heavy for old hearts to bear.

[117]But the days passed. Expectations turned into acceptance. It was the hopeless acceptance of the old, sometimes mistaken for apathy.

[118]Sometimes they hardly exchanged a word. Now they had nothing to talk about. Their days were wearing long.

[119]About a week after that, the old man woke suddenly in the night. He stretched out his hand and found himself alone.

[120]The room was in darkness. The sound of subdued weeping came from the window. Raising himself in bed, he listened.

[121]"Come back," he said tenderly. "You will be cold."

[122]"It is colder for my son," said the old woman. She wept again.

[123]The sound of her sobs died away on his ears. The bed was warm and his eyes heavy with sleep. He dozed restlessly and then slept. A sudden wild cry from his wife awoke him with a start.

[124]"The monkey's paw!" she cried wildly. "The monkey's paw!"

[125]He stared up in alarm. "Where? Where is it? What's the matter?"

[126]She came stumbling across the room toward him. "I want it," she said quietly. "You haven't destroyed it, have you?"

[127]"It's in the parlor, on the shelf over the fireplace," he replied, wondering, "Why?"

[128]She cried and laughed at the same time. Bending over, she kissed his cheek.

[129]"I only just thought of it," she said hysterically. "Why didn't I think of it before? Why didn't you think of it?"

[130]"Think of what?" he questioned.

[131]"The other two wishes," she replied rapidly. "We've only had one."

[132]"Was that not enough?" he demanded fiercely.

[133]"No," she cried in triumph. "We'll have one more. Go down and get it quickly. Wish our boy alive again."

[134]The man sat up in bed. He flung the covers from his shaking

limbs. "Good God, you are mad!" he cried, horrified.

[135]"Get it," she panted. "Get it quickly. And wish! Oh, my boy, my boy!"

[136]Her husband struck a match and lit the candle. "Get back into bed," he said trembling. "You don't know what you are saying."

[137]"We had the first wish granted," said the old woman in a feverish voice. "Why not a second one?"

[138]"A coincidence," stammered the old man.

[139]"Go and get it and wish," cried the old woman, She dragged him toward the door.

[140]He went down in the darkness and felt his way to the parlor. Then he found the mantelpiece. The talisman was in its place.

[141]He was seized by a horrible fear. What if the unspoken wish brought back his mutilated son before he could escape from the room?

[142]He caught his breath as he realized he had lost the direction of the door. His brow was cold with sweat as he felt his way round the table. He finally found himself in the small hallway with the unwholesome thing in his hand.

[143]Even his wife's face seemed changed as he entered the room. It was white and expectant. To his fearful mind, she seemed to have an unnatural look upon her face. He was afraid of her.

[144]"Wish!" she cried, in a strong voice.

[145]"It is foolish and wicked," he hesitated.

[146]"Wish!" repeated his wife.

[147]He raised his hand. "I wish my son alive again."

[148]The talisman fell to the floor, and he looked at it with horror. Then he sank trembling into a chair. But the old woman, with burning eyes, walked to the window and raised the blind.

[149]He sat until he was chilled with cold. Now and again, he glanced at the figure of the woman peering through the window.

[150]The candle had burned below the rim of the china candlestick. It threw fluttering shadows on the ceiling and walls. Finally, with a flicker larger than the rest, it expired.

[151]The old man sighed with unspeakable relief at the failure of the talisman. And he crept back to his bed.

[152]A minute or two passed. Then the old woman came silently and apathetically to bed beside him.

[153]Neither spoke. But both lay silently listening to the ticking of the clock. A stair creaked. A squeaky mouse scurried noisily through the wall.

[154]The darkness was oppressive. The husband finally screwed up his courage and took the box of matches. Striking one, he went downstairs for a candle.

[155]At the foot of the stairs the match went out. He paused to strike another. At that moment, a knock— so quiet and stealthy it was hardly heard—sounded on the front door.

[156]The matches fell from his hand. He stood motionless, holding his breath until the knock was repeated. Then he turned and fled back to his room, closing the door behind him.

[157]A third knock sounded throughout the house.

[158]"What's that?" cried the old woman, startled.

[159]"A rat," said the old man in a shaking voice. "A rat. It passed me on the stairs."

[160]His wife sat up in bed listening. A loud knock echoed through the house.

[161]"It's Herbert!" she screamed. "It's Herbert!"

[162]She ran to the door. But her husband was quicker. Catching her by the arm, he held her tightly.

[163]"What are you going to do?" he whispered hoarsely.

[164]"It's my boy. It's Herbert!" she cried, struggling. "I forgot it was two miles away. What are you holding me for? Let go. I must open the door."

[165]"For God's sake, don't let it in," cried the old man, trembling.

[166]"You're afraid of your own son," she cried, still struggling. "Let me go. I'm coming, Herbert. I'm coming."

[167]There was another knock and another. The old woman with a sudden jerk broke free and ran from the room.

[168]Her husband followed to the landing. He called after her in a pleading voice as she hurried downstairs.

[169]He heard the chain rattle back. The sound of the bottom bolt as it was pulled from its socket followed. Then came the sound of the old woman's voice, strained and panting.

[170]"The bolt," she cried loudly. "Come down. I can't reach it."

[171]But her husband was on his hands and knees on the floor, groping wildly for the paw. If he

could only find it before the thing outside got in.

[172]A thunderstorm of knocks echoed through the house. He heard the scraping of a chair as his wife put it against the door. He heard the creaking of a bolt as it came slowly back.

[173]At the same moment, he found the monkey's paw. Frantically he breathed his third and last wish.

[174]The knocking ceased suddenly, although its echoes were still in the house. He heard the chair draw back and the door opened. A cold wind rushed up the staircase.

[175]A long, loud wail of disappointment and misery from his wife gave him courage to run down to her side. From there he darted to the gate beyond. The flickering street lamp shone on a quiet and deserted road.

---

*If you have been timing your reading speed for this story, record your time below.*

_____ : _____

**Minutes      Seconds**

---

## UNDERSTANDING THE MAIN IDEA

The following questions will demonstrate your understanding of what the story is about, or the *main idea*. Choose the best answer for each question.

**1. This story is mainly about**

Ⓐ a famous monkey from India.

Ⓑ a soldier's adventures in India.

Ⓒ a family who used magic to interfere with fate.

Ⓓ how good luck charms can change someone's life.

**2. This story could have been titled**

Ⓐ "The Good Luck Charm."

Ⓑ "The Mysterious Soldier."

Ⓒ "India—That Mysterious Land."

Ⓓ "Be Careful What You Wish For."

**3. Which detail best supports the main idea of the story?**

Ⓐ Mr. White used the monkey's paw to wish for 200 pounds.

Ⓑ Herbert worked for Maw and Meggins.

Ⓒ Herbert thought he saw horrible faces in the dying fire.

Ⓓ The sergeant-major drank a glass of whiskey.

**4. Find another detail that supports the main idea of this story. Write it on the lines below.**

_____

_____

_____

## RECALLING FACTS

The following questions will test how well you remember the facts in the story you just read. Choose the best answer for each question.

**1. The Whites' first guest was**

Ⓐ a man from Maw and Meggins.

Ⓑ an expert chess player.

Ⓒ an old fakir from India.

Ⓓ a soldier Mr. White knew years ago.

**2. The monkey's paw had the power to**

Ⓐ take a person back in time.

Ⓑ stop a person from aging.

Ⓒ turn ordinary paper into giant bars of gold.

Ⓓ grant three separate men three wishes each.

**3. Rather than give the monkey's paw to Mr. White, the soldier**

Ⓐ buried it in the garden.

Ⓑ hid it in a secret place.

Ⓒ sold it to Mr. White's son.

Ⓓ threw it onto the fire.

**4. The price Mr. Morris paid for his first wish was**

Ⓐ his son's life.

Ⓑ his home.

Ⓒ his friendship with the soldier.

Ⓓ his marriage.

———— ■ ————

## READING BETWEEN THE LINES

A *theme* is a "message" found in a literary work. An *inference* is a conclusion drawn from facts. Analyze the story by choosing the best answer to each question below.

**1. A theme for this story is**

Ⓐ don't interfere with fate.

Ⓑ three wishes are never enough.

Ⓒ there are times when we can control the future.

Ⓓ magic can solve all your problems.

**2. What conclusion can you draw from paragraphs 3–11?**

Ⓐ Herbert often cheated at board games.

Ⓑ Mr. White was disgusted because he lost the chess game.

Ⓒ Mrs. White expected Herbert to always let his father win.

Ⓓ Mr. White wasn't very competitive.

**3. What conclusion can you draw from paragraphs 108–112?**

Ⓐ The visitor didn't agree with what the company was doing.

Ⓑ The visitor didn't think the Whites deserved any compensation.

Ⓒ Maw and Meggins killed Herbert on purpose.

Ⓓ The visitor disliked working with Herbert.

**4. It can be inferred from the story that**

Ⓐ Mr. and Mrs. White didn't believe in magic.

Ⓑ Herbert was in a high position with his company.

Ⓒ The soldier visited the Whites intending to give them the monkey's paw.

Ⓓ Mr. and Mrs. White loved their son very much.

## DETERMINING CAUSE AND EFFECT

Choose the best answer for the following questions to show the relationship between *what* happened in the story (*effects*) and *why* those things happened (*causes*).

1. **Because the old fakir wanted to show that fate ruled people's lives, he**

   Ⓐ put a spell on the monkey's paw.

   Ⓑ went around granting people's wishes.

   Ⓒ put a spell on the soldier.

   Ⓓ put a spell on the machinery at Maw and Meggins.

2. **What happened because Herbert was killed while at work?**

   Ⓐ His employer decided to go out of business.

   Ⓑ His employer gave the Whites 200 pounds as compensation.

   Ⓒ His employer paid for all of Herbert's funeral expenses.

   Ⓓ The Whites decided the monkey's paw was bad luck and burned it.

3. **Why did Mr. White cry out after he made his first wish?**

   Ⓐ The monkey's paw had begun to crawl across the floor.

   Ⓑ Two hundred pounds suddenly landed on his head.

   Ⓒ He felt an electric shock run through his body.

   Ⓓ The monkey's paw twisted in his hand like a snake.

4. **Why didn't Mr. White want to wish his son back to life? Answer using complete sentences.**

   _____

   _____

   _____

   _____

   _____

   _____

   ———————   ▬   ———————

## USING CONTEXT CLUES

Skilled readers can often find the meaning of unfamiliar words by using *context clues*. This means they study the way the words are used in the text. Use the context clues in the excerpts below to determine the meaning of the **bold-faced** words. Then choose the answer that best matches the meaning of the word.

**1.** "The **maligned** Mrs. White pursued him with a chair slipcover."

*CLUE*: " 'Of course,' said Herbert with pretended horror. . . . 'Wish to be an emperor to begin with, Father. Then you won't be henpecked.' Herbert darted round the table chased by his mother."

   Ⓐ ridiculed

   Ⓑ praised

   Ⓒ kind

   Ⓓ generous

**2.** "Then, with sudden **resolution**, he flung the gate open and walked up the path."

*CLUE*: "He appeared to be trying to make up his mind to enter. . . . Three times the man paused at the gate. Then he began to walk on by. The fourth time he stood with his hand upon the gate."

   Ⓐ panic

   Ⓑ impatience

   Ⓒ generosity

   Ⓓ determination

**3.** "She saw the awful **confirmation** of her fears when the man turned his face away."

*CLUE*: "She stopped suddenly as the sinister meaning of the man's words dawned upon her."

   Ⓐ recognition

   Ⓑ proof

   Ⓒ involvement

   Ⓓ denial

**4.** " 'They wish to present you with a certain sum as **compensation**.' "

*CLUE*: " 'I am to say that Maw and Meggins refuse to take any responsibility. . . . But, out of regard for your son's services, they want to make a gesture.' "

   Ⓐ payment to make up for a loss

   Ⓑ a thank you

   Ⓒ a means of punishment

   Ⓓ a method of revenge

*Nightmares and Cold Sweats*

# The Pit and the Pendulum

### Edgar Allan Poe

I was sick—sick to death from long agony. When they finally untied me and I was allowed to sit, I felt that my senses were leaving me. The sentence—the fearful sentence of death—was the last clear sound I heard.

[2] After that, the sound of the inquisitorial voices seemed to blend together in one dreamy, vague hum.

[3] This only lasted a brief time. Soon I heard no more. Yet for a while, I saw. But I saw things in an exaggerated way that was horrible!

[4] I remember seeing the lips of the black-robed judges. The lips appeared to me whiter than the paper I am writing on.

[5] I saw that the sentence that was my fate was still coming from those lips. I saw the lips twist with deadly speech. I saw them form the syllables of my name. And I trembled because there was no sound.

[6] For a few moments of feverish horror, I saw the soft and barely noticeable waving of the black drapes. These drapes wrapped the walls of the room.

[7] Then my eyes fell upon the seven tall candles on the table. At first they wore the look of kindness. They seemed like white, slender angels who would save me.

[8] But then all at once, a deadly sickness came over my spirit. I felt every nerve in my body quiver, as if I had touched an electric wire. I watched as the angel forms became ghosts with heads of flame. I saw that there would be no help from them.

[9] Then a thought crept into my mind like a rich musical note. I thought of what sweet rest there must be in the grave. The thought came gently and stealthily. It seemed a long time before I fully understood it.

[10]But just as my spirit grasped the thought, the figures of the judges disappeared, as if by magic. The tall candles sank into nothingness. The blackness of darkness followed.

[11]All feelings appeared to be swallowed up in a mad, rushing fall. It was like the descent of the soul into Hades. Then the silence and stillness and night were my universe.

[12]I had fainted. But I still do not think I lost all consciousness. What was left of it, I will not try to define or describe.

[13]Yet all was not lost. In the deepest sleep—no! In feverish insanity—no! In fainting—no! In death—no! Even in the grave, all is not lost. Otherwise, there would be no everlasting life for man.

[14]Waking up from the deepest sleep, we break the delicate web of some dream. Yet a second later (because the web is so frail), we do not remember we have dreamed.

[15]There are two stages in coming back to life after fainting. The first stage is the awakening of the mind or spirit. The second stage is physical awareness. If we could remember the first stage when we reach the second, we would probably find memories of the gulf beyond.

[16]And that gulf is—what? How, at least, do we tell its shadows from those of the tomb?

[17]Perhaps we cannot recall the first stage at will. Yet after a long time, do not the memories come to us unto their own? They flow back while we wonder in amazement where they've come from.

[18]The man who has never fainted does not find strange palaces and familiar faces in glowing coals. He does not see things floating in mid-air—the sad visions that most do not see. He does not ponder over the perfume of some new flower. He is not bewildered by some music which has never before caught his attention.

[19]Often I have tried to remember. I have struggled to recall some sign of this nothingness my soul had passed into.

[20]There have been moments when I have dreamed of success. There have been brief, very brief periods when I have brought back memories. The clear thinking of a later stage convinces me that they were from that unconscious time.

[21]These shadowy memories tell me indistinctly of tall figures that lifted me. In silence, they carried me down—down—still down. Finally a hideous dizziness overcame me at

the mere idea of how endless that descent was.

[22]The shadowy memories also tell of a vague horror I felt because of the unnatural stillness of my heart. Then everything suddenly seemed to come to a stop. It was as if this ghastly group who carried me down had gone beyond the limits of the limitless. Finally even they had to pause from their weary labor.

[23]After this I remember flatness and dampness. Very suddenly, motion and sound came back to my soul. I felt the violent motion of my heart. In my ears, I could hear it beating. Then a pause and all is blank. Then sound again and motion and touch—a tingling running through my body. Then the simple awareness, without thought, that I exist. This awareness lasted a long time.

[24]Then very suddenly, thought and terror and an attempt to understand my condition. Then a strong desire to fall back into unconsciousness. A rushing awakening of my soul and a successful effort to move my body.

[25]Now a full memory of the trial, judges, black drapes, sentence, sickness, fainting. Then discovery that I had forgotten all that followed. Time and trying to remember finally

allowed me to vaguely recall what happened.

[26]So far I had not opened my eyes. I felt that I lay on my back, untied. I reached out my hand. It fell heavily on something damp and hard. I left it there for many minutes while I tried to imagine where and what it could be.

[27]I wanted to look, but I did not dare. I dreaded the first glance at the objects around me.

[28]It was not that I was afraid to look at horrible things. But I was frightened that there would be nothing to see.

[29]Finally with wild desperation I quickly unclosed my eyes. My worst fears proved true. The blackness of endless night surrounded me.

[30]I struggled for breath. The intensity of the darkness seemed to weigh me down and strangle me. The air was intolerably stuffy.

[31]I still lay quietly and tried to think. I remembered the inquisitorial trial. From that point I tried to figure out what had happened to me.

[32]The sentence had passed. It seemed to me that a very long time had gone by since then.

[33]Yet I did not think for a moment that I was actually dead. Such a thought, no matter what we

read in fiction, cannot be true in real life. But where and in what state was I?

[34]I knew that people who are condemned to death usually perished at the autos-da-fé. One of these had been held the very evening after my trial. Had I been sent to my cell to wait for the next sacrifice, which would not take place for many months?

[35]I saw at once that this could not be. Victims were wanted immediately. Besides, my dungeon, like those of the condemned at the Toledo prison, had had stone floors. And light had not been shut out altogether.

[36]A fearful thought suddenly drove the blood in a rush to my heart. For a brief period I once more fell unconscious.

[37]When I recovered after a short time, I got to my feet at once. Every nerve in my body trembled violently. I thrust my arms wildly above and around me in all directions. I felt nothing.

[38]But still I dreaded to move a step. I feared that I might be stopped by the walls of a tomb. Sweat burst from every pore of my body. Drops stood in big, cold beads on my forehead.

[39]The agony of suspense finally grew intolerable. I cautiously moved forward with my arms extended. My eyes were straining from their sockets, hoping to see some faint ray of light.

[40]I went on for several steps. Still there was nothing but blackness and emptiness.

[41]I still continued to step cautiously forward. As I did so, I now remembered with a rush a thousand vague rumors about the horrors of Toledo. There had been strange things told about the dungeons. I had always considered them to be fables. Yet they were strange and too ghastly to repeat, except in a whisper.

[42]Was I left to perish of starvation in this underground world of darkness? Or was there some fate, perhaps even worse, that awaited me?

[43]I knew that the result would be death—and a death of more than usual bitterness. I knew my judges too well to doubt it.

[44]My outstretched hands finally touched something solid. It was a wall that seemed to be made of stone. It was very smooth, slimy, and cold.

[45]I followed this wall. But I

stepped with all care and distrust with which the old stories I had heard filled me.

[46]But this process did not allow me to find out how large my dungeon was. I could make its circuit and return to my starting point. Yet I would never realize that since the wall seemed so uniform.

[47]Therefore, I hunted for the knife which had been in my pocket when I was led into the inquisitorial chamber. But it was gone. My clothes had been exchanged for a robe of coarse, twilled fabric.

[48]I had thought of forcing the blade into some small crack of the stonework. This would have identified my starting point.

[49]The problem was minor. Nevertheless, it seemed impossible to solve at first in my confusion.

[50]Then I tore a part of the hem from my robe. I stretched out the fragment on the floor at an angle to the wall. In feeling my way around the prison, I would not fail to find the rag at the end of the circuit. Or so at least I thought.

[51]I had not counted on the large size of the dungeon or on my own weakness. The ground was moist and slippery. I staggered on for some time until I stumbled and fell.

[52]My fatigue was so great that I remained there. Sleep soon overtook me where I lay.

[53]When I woke up, I stretched out an arm. I found beside me a loaf of bread and a pitcher of water. I was too exhausted to think about this. I simply ate and drank hungrily.

[54]Shortly afterward, I began my tour around the prison again. With much effort, I at last came back to the piece of fabric. Until I had fallen, I had counted to 52 paces. When I continued my walk, I counted 48 more. Then I found the rag.

[55]There were a hundred paces in all then. Figuring that two paces equaled a yard, I guessed that the dungeon was 50 yards in circuit.

[56]However, I had found many angles in the wall. Thus I could not guess at the shape of the tomb. I could not help thinking of it as a tomb.

[57]I had little purpose—and certainly no hope—in making these researches. But a vague curiosity influenced me to continue. Leaving the wall, I decided to cross the room.

[58]At first I proceeded with extreme caution. Though the floor seemed solid, it was dangerously slimy.

[59]But finally I became brave and stepped firmly. I tried to cross in as straight a line as possible.

[60]I had advanced ten or twelve steps when the torn hem of my robe got tangled between my legs. I stepped on it and fell violently on my face.

[61]In the confusion of my fall, I failed to notice something startling. But a few seconds later while I still lay on the floor, it caught my attention.

[62]It was this: my chin rested on the floor of the prison. But the upper part of my head, though hanging lower than my chin, touched nothing. At the same time my forehead seemed bathed by a clammy vapor.

[63]The peculiar smell of rotting fungus arose to my nostrils. I reached forward. I trembled when I found that I had fallen at the very edge of a circular pit. At that moment, of course, I had no way to tell how large it was. Feeling around the stonework just below the edge, I managed to pull out a small fragment. I let it fall into the abyss.

[64]For many seconds I listened to the echoes as it dashed against the sides of the pit. Finally there was a dull plunge into water. Loud echoes followed.

[65]At the same moment I heard a sound like a door quickly opening and closing overhead. I also saw a faint gleam of light flash suddenly through the gloom. Then it faded away just as suddenly.

[66]I saw clearly the death that had been prepared for me. I congratulated myself for the timely accident that had caused me to escape. One more step and the world would have never seen me again.

[67]The kind of death I avoided was like those I heard of in tales about the Inquisition. At the time I had thought they were fables.

[68]I knew there were two possibilities for victims of the Inquisition. The condemned faced death with its most fearful physical agonies. Or they faced the most hideous mental horrors. I had been saved for the second kind.

[69]Long suffering had shattered my nerves. Now I trembled at the sound of my own voice. In every way, I had become a fitting subject for the kind of torture which awaited me.

[70]Shaking all over, I felt my way back to the wall. I decided to perish there rather than risk the terrors of the pits. I now imagined several pits around the dungeon.

[71]In a different state of mind, I

might have had the courage to end my misery. By plunging into one of these abysses, I could have ended it all.

[72]But now I was the greatest of cowards. And I could not forget what I had read about these pits. The sudden ending of life was not a part of their horrible plan.

[73]My disturbed spirit kept me awake for many long hours. Finally I fell asleep again. When I awakened, I again found a loaf of bread and a pitcher of water by my side. A burning thirst filled me. I emptied the pitcher in one gulp.

[74]It must have been drugged. I had scarcely drunk it before I became extremely drowsy.

[75]A deep sleep fell upon me—a sleep that was like death. I do not know how long it lasted, of course. But when I opened my eyes again, I could see the objects around me. The dungeon was lit by a wild, yellowish glow. At first I could not see its source.

[76]This light allowed me to see the size and appearance of the prison. I had been greatly mistaken about the size of the room. The whole circuit of its walls was not more than 25 yards.

[77]For some minutes this fact foolishly troubled me. Foolish indeed. What could be less important in this terrible situation than the mere size of my dungeon?

[78]But my mind took a wild interest in trivial matters.

[79]I had also been deceived about the shape of the dungeon. In feeling my way, I had found many angles.

[80]Thus I had formed the idea that the shape had great irregularity. That is how powerfully total darkness affects someone who is just waking up! The angles were simply a few slight nooks and crannies here and there.

[81]The general shape of the prison was square. What I had taken to be stone now seemed to be iron or some other metal. It covered the walls in huge plates. The seams where the plates were joined together formed the indented spots.

[82]The entire surface of this metal cell was crudely painted.

[83]The pictures were of hideous, disgusting design. They were of the kind that monks' superstitions about death produced. Figures of threatening demons, skeletons, and other more fearful images blotted the walls.

[84]I observed that the outlines of these monsters were distinct enough.

But the colors seemed faded and blurred, as if from damp air.

[85]I now noticed the floor too, which was of stone. In the center yawned the pit from whose jaws I had escaped. But it was the only one in the dungeon.

[86]All of this I saw indistinctly and only with much effort. This was because my position had been greatly changed during my sleep. I now lay stretched out on my back on some kind of low wooden frame. To this I was tightly tied by a long strap that looked like a saddle belt. It was wrapped many times around my limbs and body. Only my head and left arm, to some extent, remained at liberty. With much effort, I could feed myself from a clay dish that lay beside me on the floor.

[87]I saw, to my horror, that the pitcher had been removed. I say "to my horror" because I was filled with intolerable thirst. It seemed the plan of my torturers was to increase my thirst. The food in the dish was very spicy meat.

[88]Looking up, I studied the ceiling of my prison. It was some 30 or 40 feet up. It was built much like the side walls.

[89]In one of its sections, a very strange figure caught my attention.

It was the painted figure of Time as he is usually seen. But instead of a scythe, he held what seemed to be a huge pendulum. It was the same kind that is seen on old-fashioned clocks.

[90]There was something about this pendulum, however, that made me watch it more carefully. While I gazed directly up at it (because it was right above me), I imagined that I saw it move.

[91]An instant later I knew it was true. Its swing was brief and, of course, slow.

[92]I watched it for several minutes. I was somewhat fearful but more curious. Wearied at last of watching its dull movement, I looked at the other objects in the cell.

[93]A slight noise attracted my attention. Looking at the floor, I saw several enormous rats crossing it. They had come from the well that lay to my right.

[94]Even while I gazed, they came up in troops. They hurried, with ravenous eyes, drawn by the scent of the meat. It required much effort and attention to scare them away from it.

[95]A half an hour or perhaps even an hour passed. (I could not keep track of time very well.) Then I looked up again.

[96]What I saw confused and amazed me. The swing of the pendulum had increased by nearly a yard.

[97]As a result, its speed was also much greater. But what really disturbed me was that it had noticeably descended.

[98]I now saw—with horror—that the bottom formed a curved blade of glittering steel. This blade was about a foot from tip to tip. The tips pointed upward, and the lower edge seemed to be as sharp as a razor.

[99]Also like a razor, it seemed huge and heavy. The blade extended upward from the narrow edge into a solid, broad structure. It was attached to a heavy brass rod. The whole thing hissed as it swung through the air.

[100]I now knew what death had been prepared for me by the ingenuity of those monkish torturers.

[101]The inquisitors knew that I was aware of the pit. Its horrors had been saved for such a bold unbeliever as myself.

[102]I had barely avoided falling into this pit by the merest accident. I knew that surprise, or being trapped, was part of the grotesqueness of death in these dungeons.

[103]Since I had not fallen, it was not part of their devilish plan to hurl me into the abyss. Instead, a different and milder death awaited for me.

[104]Milder! I almost smiled at the use of such a word.

*The rats came in troops, drawn by the scent of the meat.*

[105]What use is it to tell of the long, long hours of cruel horror? During this time I counted the rushing swings of the steel! Inch by inch—line by line. It descended so slowly that it seemed ages before I saw a difference.

[106]Down and still down it came! Days passed! It might have been many days passed before it swept closely over me. Then as it fanned me, I felt its bitter breath. The odor of the sharp steel forced itself into my nostrils.

[107]I prayed. I wearied heaven with my plea that the pendulum would descend more quickly. I grew wild and struggled to force myself up against the fearful blade.

[108]And then I suddenly became calm. I lay smiling at the glittering death, like a child looking at some rare jewel.

[109]I had another period of total unconsciousness. It was brief, or seemed so. When I woke again there seemed to have been no perceptible descent of the pendulum.

[110]But it might have been a long period. I knew there were evil men who saw me faint. They could have stopped the pendulum's descent.

[111]When I woke up, I felt horribly sick and weak. It was as if I had been starving for a long time. Even through the agonies of that period, I still craved food.

[112]Painfully I stretched out my left arm as far as the bonds permitted. I took the small portion that the rats had spared me. As I took a bite, a half-formed thought of joy and hope rushed to my mind. Yet what business had I with hope?

[113]It was, as I said, a half-formed thought. Man has many such thoughts which are never completed. I felt it was of joy and hope. But I also felt it had died even while I was forming it.

[114]In vain I tried to bring it back and complete it. My long suffering had nearly destroyed all my ordinary mental powers. I was a fool—an idiot.

[115]The swings of the pendulum were at right angles to the length of my body. I saw that the blade was positioned to cross the area of my heart. It would tear the fabric of my robe. It would return and repeat this, again and again.

[116]The blade had a very wide sweep of about 30 feet or more. The hissing energy of its descent was enough to break even these walls of iron.

[117]Yet for several minutes, all the blade would do would be to cut my robe. And at this thought, I paused.

[118]I dared not go beyond this thought. I steadily fixed my attention on the idea. It was as if I could stop the descent of the steel by freezing my thoughts.

[119]I forced myself to ponder upon the sound of the blade as it passed across my robe. I thought about the peculiar feeling that the pull of cloth produces on the nerves. I pondered about all of these trivial things until my teeth were on edge.

[120]Down—steadily down it crept. I found mad pleasure in contrasting its speed downward with its speed from side to side.

[121]Down—certainly, relentlessly down! It swung within three inches of my chest!

[122]I struggled violently— furiously—to free my left arm. It was free only from the elbow to the hand. By working hard, I could reach from the plate to my mouth, but no farther.

[123]If I could have broken the straps about the elbow, I would have grabbed and tried to stop the pendulum. I might as well have tried to stop an avalanche!

[124]Down—still without stopping! Still constantly down! I gasped and struggled at each swing. I shrank back wildly at its every sweep. My eyes followed its outward and upward swings eagerly with despair. My eyes closed themselves when it swung down.

[125]Yet death would have been a relief. Oh, how unspeakable a relief!

[126]Still I quivered to think how small a sinking of the pendulum would bring that shining ax upon my chest. It was hope that made my nerves quiver and my body shrink. It was hope—the hope that wins out even in the midst of torture. Hope that whispers to those condemned to death, even in the dungeons of the Inquisition.

[127]I saw that just ten or twelve swings would bring the steel in contact with my robe. With this observation, my spirit was suddenly filled with the sane calmness of despair. For the first time during many hours—or perhaps days—I thought.

[128]It now occurred to me that the bandage or strap that tied me was unique. I was not tied by a separate cord. The first stroke of the razorlike blade across any part of the band would cut it. This might allow me to

use my left hand to unwind it.

[129]But how fearfully close the blade would be in that case! The result of the slightest struggle could be deadly.

[130]Dreading to kill my last hope, I raised my head to get a distinct view of my chest. The strap was tightly wrapped around my body in all directions—except in the path of the pendulum.

[131]I had scarcely dropped my head back when a thought flashed in my mind. I can only describe the idea as the unformed half of the rescue plan that I referred to earlier. Only half of the thought had floated through my brain when I raised food to my burning lips.

[132]Now the whole thought was there. It was feeble, scarcely sane, and scarcely fixed. But it was complete. I started to work at once, with the nervous energy of despair.

[133]For many hours the area around the framework upon which I lay had been swarming with rats. They were wild, bold, and ravenous. Their red eyes glared at me as if they were just waiting for me to lie motionless before they would attack. "What food," I thought, "have they been used to in the pit?"

[134]In spite of my efforts, they had eaten all but a small bit of the food in the dish. I had fallen into continually waving my hand around the plate. But after a while the movement lost its effect because it was so regular. In their greediness, they often sank their sharp fangs into my fingers.

[135]Now I took the oily, spicy meat that remained. I rubbed the strap wherever I could reach it. Then, raising my hand from the floor, I lay breathlessly still.

[136]At first the ravenous rats were terrified by the change—by the lack of movement. They shrank back in alarm. Many ran toward the pit.

[137]But this was only for a moment. I had not counted on their greediness in vain. Seeing that I was not moving, one or two of the boldest rats jumped up on the framework. They began smelling the strap.

[138]This seemed the signal for the rest to rush forward. Fresh troops hurried from the pit.

[139]They clung to the wood. They poured over it and leaped in hundreds upon me. The regular movement of the pendulum did not disturb them at all. Avoiding its strokes, they worked on the greasy strap.

[140]They pressed and swarmed on me in growing heaps. They squirmed upon my throat. Their cold lips met mine. I was half smothered by the pressure of them.

[141]Disgust that cannot be described swelled within me and chilled my heart. But I felt that in another minute the struggle would be over. I could feel the strap loosening. I knew that it must be severed already in more than one place. With a more than human strength of will, I lay still.

[142]I had not been wrong about my plan. Nor had my efforts been in vain. Finally I felt that I was free. The strap hung in shreds from my body.

[143]But the stroke of the pendulum already pressed upon my chest. It had split the fabric of my robe. It had cut through the cloth beneath. It swung twice again. A sharp pain shot through every nerve.

[144]But the moment of escape arrived. With a wave of my hand, my deliverers scuttled away. Then steadily, carefully, and slowly, I slid from the strap and away from the reach of the blade. For the moment, at least, I was free.

[145]Free! And in the grasp of the Inquisition! I had scarcely stepped away from my bed of horror when the hellish machine stopped. I saw it being pulled up through the ceiling by some invisible force.

[146]This was a lesson which I took to heart in despair. Without doubt, my every move was watched.

[147]Free! I had only escaped one form of agony, to be delivered to another that was worse than death.

[148]With that thought, I nervously looked around at the iron plates that imprisoned me. Something unusual had obviously taken place in the cell.

[149]But this change was not distinct at first. For many minutes of dreamy and trembling thought, I wondered what had happened.

[150]During this period I discovered where the yellowish light in the cell came from. It came from a crack about half an inch wide. This crack went all around the prison at the base of the walls.

[151]It appeared the walls were completely separated from the floor. I tried—in vain, of course—to look through the crack.

[152]As I got up, the mystery of the change in the cell suddenly dawned on me. I have explained that the outlines of the figures on the walls were distinct enough. Yet the colors had seemed blurred and unclear.

[153]Now these colors were becoming startlingly and intensely brilliant. This gave the ghostly, devilish portraits a look that might have frightened even someone with better nerves. Wild, ghastly demon eyes glared at me from a thousand directions where none had been visible before. They gleamed with the horrid glow of fire. I could not convince myself that this fire was unreal.

[154]Unreal! Even while I breathed, I smelled the vapor of hot iron! A choking odor filled the prison! Every second the glow in the eyes that glared at my agonies grew deeper! A richer shade of red spread over the pictures of torture.

[155]I panted! I gasped for breath! There was no doubt what my tormentors had planned. Oh, those most unrelenting, most devilish of men!

[156]I shrank from the glowing metal to the center of the cell. I thought of the fiery destruction that was near.

[157]Then the soothing idea of the coolness of the pit came over my soul. I rushed to its deadly brink. I strained my eyes below.

[158]The glare from the burning ceiling lit up the deepest corners.

Yet for a wild moment I refused to understand the meaning of what I saw. Finally it forced—it wrestled—its way into my soul. It burned itself into my trembling mind.

[159]Oh, for a voice to speak! Oh, horror! Oh, any horror but this!

[160]With a scream, I ran away from the edge. I buried my face in my hands, weeping bitterly.

[161]The heat increased rapidly. Once again I looked up, shaking as if I had a fever. There had been a second change in the cell. Now the change was obviously in the form.

[162]As before, I could not at first understand what was taking place. But I was not left in doubt for long. The Inquisition's revenge had been hurried by my two escapes. There would be no more toying with Death.

[163]The room had been square. I saw that two of its iron angles were now acute. As a result, the other two angles had become obtuse. The difference quickly increased with a low rumbling or moaning sound. Instantly the cell had become diamond-shaped.

[164]But the change did not stop here. I neither hoped nor desired it to stop. I could have embraced the red walls as a bringer of eternal peace.

[165]"Death," I said, "any death but that of the pit!"

[166]Fool! I should have known that the burning iron was supposed to force me into the pit. Could I resist its glow? Or if even that, could I withstand its pressure?

[167]And now the diamond grew flatter and flatter. This happened so rapidly that I had no time to think about it. Its center and greatest width came just over the yawning pit.

[168]I shrank back. But the closing walls pushed me forward. Finally there was not even an inch left for my burned and twisting body.

[169]I struggled no more. But my agony found release in one long, loud, and final scream. I felt myself tottering on the edge. I looked away—

[170]There was a noisy hum of human voices! There was a loud blast as of many trumpets! There was a harsh, grating sound like that of a thousand thunders!

[171]The fiery walls rushed back! An outstretched arm caught my own as I fell, fainting, into the abyss.

[172]It was General LaSalle. The French army had entered Toledo. The Inquisition was in the hands of its enemies.

---

*If you have been timing your reading speed for this story, record your time below.*

_____ : _____
**Minutes**    **Seconds**

---

## UNDERSTANDING THE MAIN IDEA

The following questions will demonstrate your understanding of what the story is about, or the *main idea*. Choose the best answer for each question.

**1. This story is mainly about**

Ⓐ the Spanish Inquisition.

Ⓑ torture chambers used throughout history.

Ⓒ the harsh life of war prisoners.

Ⓓ a man's fight to survive a torture chamber.

**2. This story could have been titled**

Ⓐ "The Survivor."

Ⓑ "The Inquisitors."

Ⓒ "Does the Punishment Fit the Crime?"

Ⓓ "War Prisoners and Their Fates."

**3. Which detail best supports the main idea of the story?**

Ⓐ The narrator used rats to help him escape the pendulum.

Ⓑ The judges had white lips.

Ⓒ The dungeon was square, with a circular pit in the center.

Ⓓ The narrator drank water that he later learned had been drugged.

**4. Find another detail that supports the main idea of this story. Write it on the lines below.**

_____

_____

_____

## RECALLING FACTS

The following questions will test how well you remember the facts in the story you just read. Choose the best answer for each question.

**1. After he was sentenced to death, the narrator**

Ⓐ tried to run away.

Ⓑ wept bitterly.

Ⓒ fainted.

Ⓓ called for help.

**2. The narrator discovered his dungeon surrounded**

Ⓐ a family of rats.

Ⓑ a circular pit.

Ⓒ a ring of fire.

Ⓓ the cells of other prisoners.

**3. Hanging from the ceiling was a**

Ⓐ swinging pendulum.

Ⓑ lantern.

Ⓒ frightening mural.

Ⓓ long rope.

**4. The narrator rubbed meat across the straps to**

Ⓐ let the grease from the meat soften them.

Ⓑ make it look like he'd eaten his dinner.

Ⓒ lure the rats into chewing the straps.

Ⓓ give himself something to do.

## READING BETWEEN THE LINES

A *theme* is a "message" found in a literary work. An *inference* is a conclusion drawn from facts. Analyze the story by choosing the best answer to each question below.

**1. A theme for this story is**

Ⓐ even when it seems like all is lost, never give up.

Ⓑ rats can sometimes be our friends.

Ⓒ someday we all must die.

Ⓓ beware of dungeons—they are full of traps!

**2. What conclusion can you draw from paragraphs 81–84?**

Ⓐ An artist had been imprisoned in that dungeon.

Ⓑ The dungeon used to be an art gallery.

Ⓒ The dungeon was a cheerful place.

Ⓓ The dungeon was an unattractive place.

**3. Write a conclusion about the narrator that can be made after reading this story. Answer using complete sentences**

_____

_____

_____

_____

_____

_____

**4. It can be inferred from the story that**

Ⓐ the narrator was saved at the end.

Ⓑ General LaSalle was an enemy of the narrator.

Ⓒ the abyss was a figment of the narrator's imagination.

Ⓓ the Inquisition was a time of great peace.

## DETERMINING CAUSE AND EFFECT

Choose the best answer for the following questions to show the relationship between *what* happened in the story (*effects*) and *why* those things happened (*causes*).

**1. Because he hadn't been put to death the night after his trial, the narrator**

Ⓐ tried to escape through an open window.

Ⓑ was convinced he'd be set free.

Ⓒ knew he would face torture.

Ⓓ begged for forgiveness.

**2. What happened because the narrator tripped over his robe?**

Ⓐ He was saved from falling into the pit.

Ⓑ The pendulum began to swing and descend.

Ⓒ The walls began closing in.

Ⓓ He was knocked unconscious.

**3. Why did the inquisitors try to kill the narrator using the pendulum instead of the pit?**

Ⓐ They knew the narrator had discovered the pit.

Ⓑ It was a new weapon, and they wanted to try it out.

Ⓒ They enjoyed watching the pendulum descend.

Ⓓ The narrator had chosen the pendulum as the way he wanted to die.

**4. Why did the inquisitors set the dungeon walls on fire?**

Ⓐ They heard General LaSalle was coming.

Ⓑ The narrator had escaped both the pit and the pendulum.

Ⓒ They wanted to scare the rats away.

Ⓓ They wanted to destroy any evidence that they had ever tortured prisoners.

## USING CONTEXT CLUES

Skilled readers can often find the meaning of unfamiliar words by using *context clues*. This means they study the way the words are used in the text. Use the context clues in the excerpts below to determine the meaning of the **bold-faced** words. Then choose the answer that best matches the meaning of the word.

**1.** "The air was **intolerably** stuffy."

*CLUE*: "I struggled for breath. The intensity of the darkness seemed to weigh me down and strangle me."

&#9312; mildly

&#9313; reasonably

&#9314; comfortably

&#9315; unbearably

**2.** "My **fatigue** was so great that I remained there."

*CLUE*: "Sleep soon overtook me where I lay."

&#9312; energy

&#9313; sorrow

&#9314; anger

&#9315; tiredness

**3.** "It now occurred to me that the bandage or strap that tied me was **unique**."

*CLUE*: "I was not tied by a separate cord. The first stroke of the razorlike blade across any part of the band would cut it."

&#9312; typical

&#9313; unusual

&#9314; strong

&#9315; fragile

**4.** "I knew that it must be **severed** already in more than one place."

*CLUE*: "I could feel the strap loosening. . . . The strap hung in shreds from my body."

&#9312; separated

&#9313; connected

&#9314; ruined

&#9315; repaired

# The Black Cat

Edgar Allan Poe

I do not expect or ask anyone to believe the wild, yet ordinary story I am about to write. I would be mad indeed to expect it. Even I cannot believe what happened. Yet I am not mad—and I know I am not dreaming. But tomorrow I die, and today I hope to unburden my soul.

[2] My main purpose is to tell the world about a series of everyday events. I tell the story plainly, briefly, and without comment. The results of these events have terrified—have tortured—have destroyed me.

[3] Yet I will not try to explain these events. To me, they have brought nothing except horror. But to many, they will seem more odd than terrifying. Perhaps later someone else will find a way to see my nightmare as ordinary. Such a person would be more calm, more logical, and far less excitable than I am. I describe these events with fear and wonder. Another might see them as just a common series of very natural causes and effects.

[4] From the time I was an infant, I was known for my obedient and kind disposition. I was so tenderhearted that my friends made fun of me.

[5] I was most fond of animals, and my parents gave me a great variety of pets. I spent most of my time with these animals. I was never happier than when I was feeding and petting them.

[6] As I grew, so did my love of animals. As an adult it was one of my main sources of pleasure. To those who have loved a faithful and wise dog, I do not need to explain how much happiness animals can bring. Something about their unselfish love goes right to the heart. This is especially true for one who has often been disappointed by the

weak friendship and loyalty of humans.

[7]I married young. I was happy to find that my wife's disposition was like mine. Seeing that I loved pets, she never passed up a chance to get the nicest kind. We had birds, goldfish, a fine dog, rabbits, a small monkey, and a cat.

[8]This cat was very large and beautiful. It was entirely black and wise beyond belief.

[9]Deep down, my wife was filled with more than a little superstition. She often mentioned the old belief that black cats are witches in disguise. Of course, she was never serious about this. I only mention the matter because I just now remembered it.

[10]Pluto—this was the cat's name—was my favorite pet and playmate. Only I fed him, and he followed me all over the house. I even had a hard time keeping him from following me through the streets.

[11]Our friendship lasted like this for several years. During this time, my personality completely changed for the worse. I am ashamed to admit it. This change happened thanks to the help of the Demon Alcohol.

[12]Day by day I grew more moody and irritable. I cared less and less about other people's feelings. I swore at my wife. Finally I even treated her violently.

[13]My pets, of course, felt the change in my disposition. I not only neglected them, but abused them. I still cared enough about Pluto to keep from mistreating him. But I did not worry about mistreating the rabbits, the monkey, or even the dog. It did not matter if they came near me by accident or for affection.

[14]My disease grew worse—for there is no disease like alcoholism! Finally even Pluto, who was growing old and cranky, began to suffer from my bad temper.

[15]One night I came home drunk from one of the places I often visited in town. I imagined that the cat was avoiding me. I grabbed him. My violence frightened him, and he nipped my hand.

[16]The fury of the demon instantly possessed me. I did not know myself. My own soul seemed to suddenly fly from my body. A devilish hatred, fed by the gin, filled me.

[17]I took a penknife from my vest pocket, opened it, and grabbed the poor cat by the throat. Then I deliberately cut one of its eyes from the socket! I blush, I burn, I shudder

while I write about this damnable atrocity.

[18]The next morning I could think more clearly, since I had slept off the drunkenness of the night before. I felt half horrified and half sorry for my crime.

[19]It was a weak and mixed feeling at best. I did not regret it deep down in my soul. I began to drink too much again. Soon I drowned the memory of what I had done in wine.

[20]In the meantime the cat slowly recovered. It is true that the socket of the lost eye looked frightful. Yet he no longer seemed to be in any pain. He went about the house as usual. But, as might be expected, he fled in terror when I came near.

[21]Some of my old feelings still remained. So I felt hurt because the creature who once loved me now clearly disliked me. But soon this feeling changed to irritation. And then, as if to defeat me once and for all, came the spirit of PERVERSENESS.

[22]No thought is given to this spirit. Yet just as I am sure that my soul lives, I am sure that perverseness is one of the basic urges of the human heart. It is one

*Finally even Pluto began to suffer from his owner's bad temper.*

of the primary emotions that shapes a person's character.

[23]Who has not, a hundred times, found himself doing a shameful or

stupid deed just because he knows he should not? Aren't we always inclined to disobey the Law, just because we know it is the Law? And we do this in spite of our better judgment.

[24]As I said, this spirit of perverseness finally defeated me. My soul longed to torment itself—to be violent to itself—to do wrong just for the sake of doing wrong.

[25]This mysterious longing urged me to continue and finally to finish the injury to the innocent brute. One morning in cold blood, I slipped a noose about its neck and hung it from the limb of a tree. I hung it with tears streaming from my eyes and with bittersweet remorse.

[26]I hung it because I knew that it had loved me and because I knew that I was committing a sin—a sin so deadly that I might risk losing my immortal soul. Even the Most Merciful and Most Fearful God might not be able to save me.

[27]The night after I had done this most cruel deed, I was awakened by the cry of fire. The curtains around my bed were in flames. The whole house was blazing.

[28]My wife, a servant, and I escaped from the raging fire with great difficulty. The destruction was complete. Everything I owned was swallowed up. From that point on I gave in to despair.

[29]I am not so foolish as to look for a link between the disaster and my atrocity. But I am giving the details about a chain of facts. I do not wish to leave out any possible link.

[30]On the day after the fire I visited the ruins of my house. All of the walls except one had fallen in. This one wall was not very thick and stood in about the middle of the house. The head of my bed had rested against it.

[31]For the most part, the plastering here had withstood the fire. I guessed that this was because the plaster had been spread recently.

[32]A dense crowd of people were gathered around this wall. Many of them seemed to be examining a part of it very closely and eagerly. The words *strange! odd!* and other expressions made me curious. I came closer and saw in the white plaster the outline of a huge cat. It was amazing how accurate the image was. There was a rope about the animal's neck.

[33]When I first saw this ghost— I could hardly consider it as any less—my wonder and my terror were extreme. As I thought about what must have happened, I was

calmed. I remembered that the cat had hung in a garden next to the house. When the fire was discovered, this garden had been filled immediately by the crowd. Someone must have cut down the animal from the tree. Then that person probably threw the body through an open window into my bedroom. This had probably been done to wake me up.

[34]When the other walls fell, the cat's body had been pressed into the fresh plaster. Then the lime from the plaster, with the flames and ammonia from the carcass, had made the image I saw.

[35]I reasoned through the events this way. But I was not completely satisfied. The startling image still made a deep impression on me. For months I could not forget the vision of the cat.

[36]During this time I felt something that seemed like remorse but was not. I went so far as to regret the loss of the animal. In the disgusting places I often visited, I searched for another animal that looked the same to take its place.

[37]One night I sat, half drunk, in a tavern known for wickedness. I suddenly saw a black object. It was lying on top of one of the huge barrels of gin or rum. These were the main pieces of furniture in the room. I had been staring at this barrel for some minutes. Therefore, I was surprised that I had not seen the object sooner.

[38]I approached it and touched it with my hand. It was a black cat—a very large one. It was easily as large as Pluto and looked like him in every way but one. Pluto hadn't had a white hair on any part of his body. But this cat had a large, shapeless splotch of white. This splotch covered nearly all of its breast.

[39]When I touched him, he immediately stood up and purred loudly. He rubbed against my hand and seemed delighted with my attention.

[40]This was the very creature I had been searching for. I offered at once to buy it from the landlord. He claimed it was not his—knew nothing about it—had never seen it before.

[41]I continued to pet the animal. When I started to go home, it acted like it wanted to follow me. I let it do so. Sometimes I would stoop down and pat it as I walked.

[42]When it reached the house, it made itself at home at once. It immediately became a great favorite with my wife. As for me, I soon found myself disliking it. This was just the opposite of what I had

expected. I do not know why, but its fondness for me disgusted and annoyed me. Slowly, these feelings of disgust and annoyance grew into bitter hatred. I avoided the creature.

[43]A sense of shame and the memory of my former cruelty kept me from physically abusing it. For some weeks I did not strike or treat it violently. But gradually—very gradually—I came to view it with more loathing than words can tell. I fled silently when I saw it, as if from some terrible disease.

[44]I had made a discovery that added to my hatred for the beast. On the morning after I brought it home, I found that it was missing an eye like Pluto. This only made my wife love the cat more. As I have already said, my wife was gentle and tenderhearted—as I had once been.

[45]The more I hated this cat, though, the more it seemed to like me. I cannot describe how stubbornly it followed my footsteps. Whenever I sat down, it would crouch under my chair. Or it would spring up on my knees and smother me with its awful affection.

[46]If I got up to walk, it would get between my feet and almost trip me. Or it would fasten its long, sharp claws in my clothes and climb up to my chest.

[47]At these times I longed to kill it with a single blow. I was kept from doing so, partly by the memory of my former crime. But mainly I was prevented—let me confess it at once—by my deep dread of the beast.

[48]This was not exactly a dread of physical evil. Yet I do not know how else to explain it. Even now in my prison cell I am almost ashamed. It is difficult for me to admit why my terror and horror grew. It was one of the silliest ideas one could imagine.

[49]My wife had called my attention, more than once, to the splotch of white hair I had mentioned. That was the only visible difference between this strange beast and the one I had destroyed.

[50]The reader will remember that, though this mark was large, it had been shapeless. But slowly—so slowly that I thought I was imagining it—the outline had finally become very clear. It now looked like an object that I shudder to name.

[51]This object, above all, made me hate and dread the monster. I would have gotten rid of it had I dared. The white patch was now the image of an awful—of a ghastly thing! It was the GALLOWS!—the sad and terrible machine of Horror and of Crime, of Agony, and of Death!

[52]And now I was truly miserable beyond the misery of ordinary humanity. Here was this brute beast—like the one I had destroyed—giving me such grief! Me—a man made in the image of God.

[53]Alas! I could not rest by day or night. During the day the creature did not leave me alone. And at night I awoke every hour from fearful dreams to find the hot breath of the thing upon my face. It was a living nightmare that I could not shake off—a huge weight forever upon my heart!

[54]Under the pressure of these torments, the last little bit of good within me disappeared. Evil thoughts became my only friends—the darkest and most evil of thoughts. My usual moodiness increased until I hated everything and everyone. I did not even try to control my many sudden outbursts of anger. My uncomplaining wife was usually the victim of my fury.

[55]One day she went with me on some household errand into the cellar. Because we were so poor, we were forced to live in an old building.

[56]The cat followed me down the steep stairs. When it nearly tripped me, it enraged me to the point of madness.

[57]I picked up an axe. In my anger, I forgot the childish fear that had kept me from doing this before. I aimed a blow at the animal. This blow, of course, would have been instantly fatal had it landed as I wished. But my wife jumped in and stopped the blow with her hand.

[58]Her interference drove me into an evil rage. I jerked my arm from her grasp and buried the axe in her brain. She fell dead on the spot without a groan.

[59]This gruesome murder done, I began at once to think carefully of how to hide the body. I knew I could not take it out of the house either by day or by night. I would risk being seen by the neighbors.

[60]Many ideas came to my mind. At one time I thought of cutting the body into little fragments and destroying them by fire. At another time I decided to dig a grave for the body in the floor of the cellar.

[61]Again I thought about throwing it in the well in the yard. Then I considered packing it in a box as if it were a package to mail. I would get a deliveryman to take it from the house.

[62]Finally I hit upon what I considered a far better idea. I decided to wall the body up in the cellar, as the monks of the Middle

Ages are said to have walled up their victims.

[63]The cellar was perfect for this purpose. Its walls were loosely built and had lately been plastered. The rough plaster had not hardened because the cellar was so damp.

[64]Also a false chimney or fireplace jutted out from one of the walls. It had been filled up and made to look like the rest of the cellar. I was sure that I could easily take out the bricks from this place. I could insert the body and wall up the whole thing as it was before. I was certain I could do it so that no one who looked at the wall would suspect anything.

[65]I was right about this plan. Using a crowbar, I easily removed the bricks. I carefully stood the body against the inner wall and propped it in place. I relaid the bricks as they had been before. With mortar, sand, and hair, I made a plaster just like the old. I very carefully went over the new brickwork with this mixture.

[66]When I had finished, I felt satisfied that everything looked right. The wall gave no hint that it had been disturbed. I picked up the trash on the floor very carefully. I looked around with a feeling of success. Then I said to myself, "Here, at least,

my labor has not been useless."

[67]My next step was to look for the beast that had been the cause of so much misery. I had, at last, firmly decided to put it to death. There is no doubt what its fate would have been had I found it at the time. But the clever animal, it seemed, had been alarmed by my violence. It chose not to be around me in my present mood.

[68]It is impossible to describe or imagine how happy and relieved I felt when the hateful creature was absent. It did not appear during the night. So I slept soundly and peacefully for the first time since the beast had followed me home. Yes, slept, even with the burden of murder on my soul.

[69]The second and the third day passed. Still my tormentor did not come. Once again I began to feel like a free man. The monster, in terror, had fled the house forever! I would never see it again! My happiness was supreme!

[70]The guilt of my dark deed hardly bothered me. A few questions had been asked, but I had easily answered them. A search had been started, but of course nothing was found. I thought my future happiness was safe.

[71]On the fourth day after the murder the police came to the house without warning. They started once more to carefully search the property. I was confident about the secrecy of my hiding place. I did not feel embarrassed at all.

[72]The officers told me to come with them as they searched. They left no corner unexplored. Finally for the third or fourth time they went down into the cellar.

[73]I did not tremble in the least. My heart beat as calmly as a person sleeping in innocence. I walked the cellar from end to end. I folded my arms on my chest and roamed easily around.

[74]The police were completely satisfied and prepared to leave. My happiness was too strong to keep inside. I wanted to say even just one word in victory to make them more sure that I was not guilty.

[75]"Gentlemen," I said at last as they went up the stairs, "I am glad to have eased your doubts. May you all be healthy and a little more courteous.

[76]"By the way, gentlemen, this—this is a very well-built house." (In the mad desire to say something casually, I hardly knew what I said at all.)

[77]"I may say this is an excellently well-built house. These walls—are you going, gentlemen?—these walls are solidly built."

[78]And here, through the excitement of bravado, I rapped my cane on the wall heavily. I hit the very spot of brickwork that hid my dead wife's body.

[79]But may God protect and save me from the fangs of the Devil! No sooner had the echo of my blows faded than I was answered by a voice from within the tomb! It was a cry!

[80]At first it was soft and broken, like the sobbing of a child. Then quickly it swelled into one long, loud, and continuous scream. It was totally unnatural and inhuman. It was a howl, a wailing shriek, half of horror and half of victory. Such a sound could have only come straight from the throats of the damned in hell and of the demons rejoicing at their pain.

[81]It is foolish to speak of my own thoughts. Feeling faint, I staggered to the wall on the other side of the room. For one instant, the group on the stairs stood frozen in fear. Then a dozen strong arms tore at the wall. It fell.

[82]There the corpse stood before

our eyes. It was already greatly decayed and covered with gore. On its head, with an open, red mouth and one single eye of fire, sat the beast. It was the same horrible animal whose craft had tricked me into murder. Its voice had informed the police and condemned me to the hangman. I had walled the monster up within the tomb.

*If you have been timing your reading speed for this story, record your time below.*

_____ : _____

**Minutes**     **Seconds**

## UNDERSTANDING THE MAIN IDEA

The following questions will demonstrate your understanding of what the story is about, or the *main idea*. Choose the best answer for each question.

**1. This story is mainly about**

Ⓐ a cat that saved his owner's life.

Ⓑ how pets give humans unselfish love.

Ⓒ a gentle man who became a violent alcoholic.

Ⓓ a couple who opened their home to stray animals.

**2. This story could have been titled**

Ⓐ "The Cat Lover."

Ⓑ "The Tenderhearted Couple."

Ⓒ "The Care and Feeding of Cats."

Ⓓ "The Man Who Became a Monster."

**3. Which detail best supports the main idea of the story?**

Ⓐ One night while drinking, the narrator killed his favorite pet.

Ⓑ The narrator's wife, like her husband, loved animals.

Ⓒ The couple lost their home and their possessions in a fire.

Ⓓ The narrator's friends made fun of his kind nature when he was young.

**4. Find another detail that supports the main idea of this story. Write it on the lines below.**

_____

_____

_____

## RECALLING FACTS

The following questions will test how well you remember the facts in the story you just read. Choose the best answer for each question.

**1. The narrator's favorite pet was**

Ⓐ a black cat.

Ⓑ a goldfish.

Ⓒ a canary.

Ⓓ a pony.

**2. As he sank into alcoholism, the narrator became**

Ⓐ sad and lonely.

Ⓑ timid and quiet.

Ⓒ mean and violent.

Ⓓ silly and clumsy.

**3. After the fire, the strange image left on the wall was the outline of**

Ⓐ a cat with a white splotch on its chest.

Ⓑ the narrator's wife.

Ⓒ a cat with a rope around its neck.

Ⓓ the narrator as a young boy.

**4. The narrator murdered his wife when she**

Ⓐ tried to stop him from hurting their cat.

Ⓑ wouldn't stop nagging him about his drinking.

Ⓒ threatened to give away all of their pets.

Ⓓ confessed to setting their house on fire.

## READING BETWEEN THE LINES

A *theme* is a "message" found in a literary work. An *inference* is a conclusion drawn from facts. Analyze the story by choosing the best answer to each question below.

**1. A theme for this story is**

(A) crime doesn't pay.

(B) cats make loyal pets.

(C) alcohol can bring out the worst in people.

(D) animals are better companions than people.

**2. What conclusion can you draw from paragraph 6?**

(A) In the past, humans had let the narrator down.

(B) The narrator preferred to spend his time with large groups of people.

(C) The narrator didn't have a lot of patience with animals.

(D) The narrator wanted to work at zoo.

**3. What conclusion can you draw from paragraph 66?**

(A) The narrator needed only a few hours of sleep per night.

(B) The narrator was blinded by grief over his wife's death.

(C) The shame of his actions was more than the narrator could stand.

(D) The narrator was unemotional about murdering his wife.

**4. It can be inferred from the story that**

(A) the narrator was arrested for murdering his wife.

(B) the wife's superstitions about black cats were real.

(C) the second black cat didn't know what happened to Pluto.

(D) the wife drank as much as her husband.

## DETERMINING CAUSE AND EFFECT

Choose the best answer for the following questions to show the relationship between *what* happened in the story (*effects*) and *why* those things happened (*causes*).

1. **Because the narrator and his wife loved animals, they**

   Ⓐ decided not to have children.

   Ⓑ owned several pets.

   Ⓒ moved to a farm.

   Ⓓ opened a pet store.

2. **What happened because the narrator became an alcoholic?**

   Ⓐ His personality changed from tenderhearted to violent.

   Ⓑ His wife left him.

   Ⓒ All of his pets ran away from him.

   Ⓓ He lost his job.

3. **Why did the narrator hang his cat?**

   Ⓐ He longed to do wrong for the sake of doing wrong.

   Ⓑ He had become allergic to it.

   Ⓒ His wife threatened to leave him if he didn't do it.

   Ⓓ The cat had become mean in his old age.

4. **Why did the narrator hate the splotch of white hair on his second cat?**

   Ⓐ It made him miss his first cat.

   Ⓑ It was in the shape of a gallows.

   Ⓒ It was impossible to keep clean.

   Ⓓ It looked like his wife's face.

———■———

*Nightmares and Cold Sweats*

## USING CONTEXT CLUES

Skilled readers can often find the meaning of unfamiliar words by using *context clues*. This means they study the way the words are used in the text. Use the context clues in the excerpts below to determine the meaning of the **bold-faced** words. Then choose the answer that best matches the meaning of the word.

**1.** "From the time I was an infant, I was known for my obedient and kind **disposition**."

*CLUE*: "I was so tenderhearted that my friends made fun of me."

   Ⓐ meanspiritedness

   Ⓑ family

   Ⓒ friends

   Ⓓ personality

**2.** "But gradually—very gradually—I came to view it with more **loathing** than words can tell."

*CLUE*: "I fled silently when I saw it, as if from some terrible disease."

   Ⓐ impatience

   Ⓑ curiosity

   Ⓒ disgust

   Ⓓ admiration

**3.** "Her **interference** drove me into an evil rage."

*CLUE*: "This blow, of course, would have been instantly fatal had it landed as I wished. But my wife jumped in and stopped the blow with her hand."

   Ⓐ assistance

   Ⓑ interruption

   Ⓒ anger

   Ⓓ ignorance

**4.** "And here, through the excitement of **bravado**, I rapped my cane on the wall heavily." (paragraph 78)

Write what you think the **bold-faced** word means. Then record the context clues that led you to this definition.

Meaning:

_____

_____

_____

Context Clues:

_____

_____

_____

———■———

# End-of-Unit Activities

1. The *climax* of a story is the turning point. It is the
   moment of highest intensity.and interest. Choose two
   stories from Unit Three, "A Surplus of Horror." Fill out the
   plotlines below, labeling what the climax was in each
   story. Then decide which story you think had a better
   climax. Describe why you think that story's climax was
   better on the lines below.

**Story 1** _____

Climax:_____

_____

_____

**Story 2** _____

Climax:_____

_____

_____

Better Climax: _____

_____

_____

_____

_____

*Nightmares and Cold Sweats*

# End-of-Unit Activities

2. **Rank each of the stories in this unit, from the one you liked the most to the one you liked the least. Then write a paragraph describing why you liked the story you ranked *1* the best.**

**LESSON 9** Ranking _____

_____

_____

_____

_____

**LESSON 10** Ranking _____

_____

_____

_____

_____

**LESSON 11** Ranking _____

_____

_____

_____

_____

**LESSON 12** Ranking _____

_____

_____

_____

_____

Why did you like the story you ranked *1* the best?

_____

_____

_____

_____

*Nightmares and Cold Sweats*

# Words-Per-Minute Chart

## UNIT THREE

**Directions:**

Use the chart to find your words-per-minute reading speed. Refer to the reading time you recorded at the end of each story. Find your reading time in seconds along the left-hand side of the chart or minutes and seconds along the right-hand side of the chart. Your words-per-minute score will be listed next to the time in the column below the appropriate lesson number.

Seconds

Minutes and Seconds

| No. of Words | Lesson 9 4,775 | Lesson 10 3,919 | Lesson 11 5,535 | Lesson 12 3,588 | |
|---|---|---|---|---|---|
| 360 | 796 | 653 | 923 | 598 | 6:00 |
| 380 | 754 | 619 | 874 | 567 | 6:20 |
| 400 | 716 | 588 | 830 | 538 | 6:40 |
| 420 | 682 | 560 | 791 | 513 | 7:00 |
| 440 | 651 | 534 | 755 | 489 | 7:20 |
| 460 | 623 | 511 | 722 | 468 | 7:40 |
| 480 | 597 | 490 | 692 | 449 | 8:00 |
| 500 | 573 | 470 | 664 | 431 | 8:20 |
| 520 | 551 | 452 | 639 | 414 | 8:40 |
| 540 | 531 | 435 | 615 | 399 | 9:00 |
| 560 | 512 | 420 | 593 | 384 | 9:20 |
| 580 | 494 | 405 | 573 | 371 | 9:40 |
| 600 | 478 | 392 | 554 | 359 | 10:00 |
| 620 | 462 | 379 | 536 | 347 | 10:20 |
| 640 | 448 | 367 | 519 | 336 | 10:40 |
| 660 | 434 | 356 | 503 | 326 | 11:00 |
| 680 | 421 | 346 | 488 | 317 | 11:20 |
| 700 | 409 | 336 | 474 | 308 | 11:40 |
| 720 | 398 | 327 | 461 | 299 | 12:00 |
| 740 | 387 | 318 | 449 | 291 | 12:20 |
| 760 | 377 | 309 | 437 | 283 | 12:40 |
| 780 | 367 | 301 | 426 | 276 | 13:00 |
| 800 | 358 | 294 | 415 | 269 | 13:20 |
| 820 | 349 | 287 | 405 | 263 | 13:40 |
| 840 | 341 | 280 | 395 | 256 | 14:00 |
| 860 | 333 | 273 | 386 | 250 | 14:20 |
| 880 | 326 | 267 | 377 | 245 | 14:40 |
| 900 | 318 | 261 | 369 | 239 | 15:00 |
| 920 | 311 | 256 | 361 | 234 | 15:20 |
| 940 | 305 | 250 | 353 | 229 | 15:40 |
| 960 | 298 | 245 | 346 | 224 | 16:00 |
| 980 | 292 | 240 | 339 | 220 | 16:20 |
| 1,000 | 287 | 235 | 332 | 215 | 16:40 |
| 1,020 | 281 | 231 | 326 | 211 | 17:00 |
| 1,040 | 275 | 226 | 319 | 207 | 17:20 |
| 1,060 | 270 | 222 | 313 | 203 | 17:40 |
| 1,080 | 265 | 218 | 308 | 199 | 18:00 |
| 1,100 | 260 | 214 | 302 | 196 | 18:20 |
| 1,120 | 256 | 210 | 297 | 192 | 18:40 |
| 1,140 | 251 | 206 | 291 | 189 | 19:00 |
| 1,160 | 247 | 203 | 286 | 186 | 19:20 |
| 1,180 | 243 | 199 | 281 | 182 | 19:40 |
| 1,200 | 239 | 196 | 277 | 179 | 20:00 |
| 1,220 | 235 | 193 | 272 | 176 | 20:20 |
| 1,240 | 231 | 190 | 268 | 174 | 20:40 |
| 1,260 | 227 | 187 | 264 | 171 | 21:00 |
| 1,280 | 224 | 184 | 259 | 168 | 21:20 |
| 1,300 | 220 | 181 | 255 | 166 | 21:40 |
| 1,320 | 217 | 178 | 252 | 163 | 22:00 |
| 1,340 | 214 | 175 | 248 | 161 | 22:20 |
| 1,360 | 211 | 173 | 244 | 158 | 22:40 |
| 1,380 | 208 | 170 | 241 | 156 | 23:00 |
| 1,400 | 205 | 168 | 237 | 154 | 23:20 |
| 1,420 | 202 | 166 | 234 | 152 | 23:40 |
| 1,440 | 199 | 163 | 231 | 150 | 24:00 |

*Nightmares and Cold Sweats*